July 13, 1985

30

— A Maverick Publication —

Oregon's Great Basin Country

by
Denzel Ferguson
and
Nancy Ferguson

Library of Congress Catalog Card Number 78-66929

ISBN 0-89288-33-3   Third Printing—April 1982

published by
Maverick Publications
Drawer 5007 • Bend, Oregon 97701

Contents

Foreword

We have had the good fortune of living in southeastern Oregon for nearly six years. Now we *expect* the coyotes to serenade us each evening, the sandhill cranes to greet us each morning with strident calls, and Nuttall's cottontails to nibble the grasses near our doorsteps. Although we will never take them for granted, we have learned to contain our enthusiasm for the magnificent contrasts between the salt-encrusted expanse of the Alvord Desert and the lofty and colorful grandeur of Steens Mountain. We have happened upon hot springs, abandoned hamlets, rimrocks, vistas, and many of the area's plants and creatures. It has been a special joy.

Now many people are discovering Oregon's Great Basin country, and each year we have had the pleasure of meeting several thousands of these excited visitors. They are hungry for more information about the area. Having had the tremendous benefit of hearing questions people were asking, we decided we might be able to put their requests and needs into one handy reference.

Many friends and acquaintances gave encouragement and assistance. To all of them, we extend our gratitude. But Carroll Littlefield, Bruce Nolf, Caryn Talbot, and Karl Urban read the manuscript, made excellent suggestions, and deserve special recognition for their contributions. Esther Gruber drew the map; James Burgess advised us about photographs. To all of these beautiful people we owe a great deal.

Although this book may be of interest to a wide audience of students, teachers, and friends of the basin area, it was designed to assist and encourage the first time visitor. The book can be read before or after a trip to Oregon's Great Basin country, but we hope it will be part of the essential travel gear and serve as a trusted reference, guide, and companion. We hope the book will intensify, clarify, and enrich the fantastic experiences that await those who would come see the high desert. We would be absolutely delighted if the book turned out to be a bit of frosting on what is unquestionably one of Nature's finest cakes.

Malheur Field Station   Denzel Ferguson
Burns, Oregon 97720   Nancy Ferguson
29 January 1978

CHAPTER 1

The Northern Great Basin

The Great Basin has contributed wild and exciting chapters to Western history—exploration and discovery, gold rushes, travel through hostile lands, cattle barons, construction of transcontinental railroads, and many others. Despite past activities in the area, vast portions of the Great Basin remain relatively undisturbed by man, although the grazing of livestock has affected even the most remote places. Today, the human population is sparse, towns are mostly rural, small, and widely dispersed, and large areas remain roadless and far from railroad services. In the Great Basin, modern technology is secondary to wildlife, open range, feral horses, buckaroos, and other vestiges of the old West.

The Great Basin is primarily an extensive intermountain plateau. It occupies about 190,000 square miles of the western United States, including portions of California, Oregon, Idaho, Utah, and all but the southern tip of Nevada. Boundaries of the basin are formed by the Sierra Nevada Range, Klamath River Drainage, Columbia Plateau, Wasatch Range, Colorado Plateau, and San Bernadino Mountains. Such widely separated localities as Burns (Oregon), Ogden (Utah), the Salton Sea, and Lake Tahoe are included.

Internal drainage is the most distinctive feature of the Great Basin, and the entire region is part of the larger Basin and Range Province, which is characterized by numerous fault-block mountain ranges rising above surrounding plateaus and valleys. In the Great Basin, fault-block ranges, created by large scale vertical displacements of the earth's crust, tend to be oriented on a north-south axis. These mountain ranges are commonly 50 to 75 miles long, 6 to 15 miles wide, and reach elevations of 7,000 to 12,000 feet. Between the mountains lie intermontane basins, actually expansive high plains in most areas, having no outlet to the ocean. In these basins of internal drainage, called bolsons, trapped water can only flow to the lowest point (the Great Salt Lake and its basin constitute a bolson). Throughout the Great Basin, many streams flow intermittently and often terminate in shallow, saline lakes, many of which evaporate to expose playas during the dry season. Other former lake beds are now dry.

Because the Great Basin is cut off from marine sources of moisture by the Cascade and Sierra Nevada ranges, the region is extremely arid. Annual precipitation seldom exceeds 10 inches and is often less than five inches at lower elevations. No comparably sized area of the United States receives less precipitation. Humidity is low, evaporation extreme, and cloud cover minimal (e.g., Nevada has an average of 193 clear days per year). In the northern portions of the Great Basin, summer temperatures are moderate, seldom exceeding 90°F, but winter temperatures are harsh with record lows around -35°F. Toward the south, summer temperatures become extreme and winters mild.

Although some mountain peaks in the Great Basin exceed 13,000 feet and Death Valley extends 282 feet below sea level, most of the area ranges from 4,000 to 6,000 feet in elevation and is relatively flat, with the eastern and northern portions being generally higher. Where erosion has sculpted the landscape, cliffs, steep slopes, and stark mesas have resulted. These abrupt features contrast strikingly with the more gentle terrain found in humid climates.

Because of deficient moisture and intense evaporation, trees are confined to higher elevations. In the northern portion of the Great Basin, an area sometimes called the high desert or cold desert, sagebrush and associated species such as greasewood, rabbitbrush, and shadscale are monotonously predominant. The name "Sagebrush Country" has been used as an apt synonym for "Great Basin". About two-thirds of the way down Nevada the low desert or hot desert appears, and creosote, various cacti, and Joshua trees take over, and sagebrush and other species typical of more northern regions persist only at higher elevations. Growing season (the frost free season) varies from fewer than 60 days at high elevations to around 250 days in the south.

The Great Basin is a desert. Although definitions may differ, the essential feature of a desert is that potential evaporation is usually 7 to 50 times greater than precipitation. Evaporation is greatest in the south (e.g., 141 inches per year at Clay City, Nevada), but may exceed precipitation by only four times in the northern parts of the cold desert. In such environments, water loss from plants is potentially catastrophic. Shallow, porous soils containing little organic matter are unable to retain available water. Because of competition for water, desert plants are widely spaced, leaving soils exposed to the forces of rains, which may be torrential in thunderstorms, and winds, which may be locally strong accompanying frontal movements. Thus, the desert is an enigma, simultaneously harsh and fragile.

2

This book deals primarily with the northern reaches of the Great Basin, that portion of the high desert in Oregon and south to near the vicinity of Winnemucca, Nevada. Although the remaining chapters specifically apply to this area, much of the information is valid for the remainder of the high desert, and therefore, to most of the Great Basin south to the latitude of Tonopah, Nevada.

CHAPTER 2

Geology

The geological history of the Great Basin is a story of fantastic changes—changes in structure and shape of the land, in the climate, and in the plants and animals. There have been periods when oceans inundated the land, and times when the climate turned subtropical or tropical. Huge mountain ranges have risen, only to be obliterated by the forces of erosion. Plants and animals, known only from fossils, have dominated exotic landscapes that would be completely foreign to the modern observer. Deciduous and coniferous forests have thrived where the land is now bleak, dry, and inundated by drifting sand. What forces brought about such drastic changes?

There was a time when marine seas periodically occupied much of the present Great Basin. Within the last 200-250 million years, uplift and other geological processes were laying the foundations for the great mountain systems of western North America. By some 60 million years ago the continent had assumed approximately its present general shape. Since then, folding, faulting, and volcanism produced the Coast Ranges, Cascades, Sierra Nevadas, and Rockies. Continuing uplift and volcanism have elevated these ranges even to recent times. Once these great barriers were in place, they intercepted moisture-laden air masses coming off the Pacific Ocean. The vast interior region was encircled, deprived of precipitation, and on its way to becoming the Great Basin.

The oldest exposed rocks in southeastern Oregon occur in the Trout Creek and Pueblo mountains, where partially metamorphosed, sedimentary and volcanic rocks of the late Paleozoic or Mesozoic eras (about 190-250 million years old) are found.

The geological history of Steens Mountain in southeastern Oregon is somewhat typical of events that have formed the basin region.

Exposed at low elevation on the east side of Steens Mountain is a layer of sedimentary rock derived from volcanic material, principally cinder and ash. These deposits called the Alvord Creek Formation, are late Miocene or Pliocene in age. They contain fossil maples, conifers, and other plants suggesting that the area received about twice the current annual rainfall and that temperatures were milder with less drastic extremes. Above these fossil-bearing deposits is a sequence of volcanic rocks, as much as 1,500 feet thick, called the Pike Creek Formation. Included in this zone are layers of volcanic ash (tuff), pink and reddish-brown rhyolite, thunderegg deposits, and other materials. Above the Pike Creek volcanics is a zone several thousand feet thick of poorly stratified flows and breccias (cemented angular fragments) of andesite and basalt called (by some authors) the Steens Mountain Volcanic Series. Finally, atop all this, lie mid-to late Miocene (15 million years ago) flows of Steens Basalt. As many as 70 separate flows can be counted, each averaging about 10 feet in thickness, but ranging from one foot to more than 70 feet. The total accumulation exceeds 3,000 feet, even today after considerable erosion has taken place. Layers of welded tuff (Danforth Formation) came later (about 6 to 9 million years ago) and are currently seen exposed in rims between Frenchglen and Burns, west of Steens Mountain.

Flows of Steens Basalt occurred at about the same time as the more famous Columbia River Basalt flows, father north, in the Columbia Basin. The two lavas are related, but can be easily distinguished by the presence of large phenocrysts (i.e., embedded crystals) in the Steens Basalt. Steens Basalt spread widely over the plateaus of southeastern Oregon, and related lavas covered Abert Rim and the Owyhee uplands. Although Steens Basalt flowed to the base of the Trout Creek Mountains, that range was not covered. The lava issued forth from magma reservoirs deep in the earth, escaped from fissures (dikes), many of which are visible on the east side of Steens Mountain, and then flowed over the surrounding plateau. Intercalated between the lava layers are ash deposits and thin layers of sedimentary material, representing intervals of disrupted flow and other geological activity. These vast flows probably erupted within a relatively short time—perhaps within 50,000 years.

Although the High Lava Plains and Cascades near Bend offer some of the freshest volcanic landscape in Oregon, excellent examples of major volcanic features and processes are readily available in southeastern Oregon. Diamond Craters volcanic field, south of Princeton, includes cinder cones, pit craters, lava flows, and lava tubes. Malheur Cave is a classic example of a large lava tube cave. Obsidian or volcanic glass is abundant near Glass Butte (east of Hampton), near Hines, and elsewhere. Obsidian artifacts of Great Basin Indians are everywhere to be found. Extensive units of young lava occur east of Andrews, near Arock, and in other localities.

While the Great Basin was being elevated, north-south oriented fractures developed in the crust, and in many instances, vertical displacements of large blocks of the earth's crust occurred along these faults.

In southeastern Oregon an extensive upland plateau composed of thousands of feet of rock, as described earlier, existed at the present site of Steens Mountain. A fracture developed along what is now the eastern base of the Steens, and repeated uplift along that fault (beginning perhaps 10 million years ago) left the crest of the fault block about 5,500 feet (more before erosion) above the Alvord Basin to the east. The scarp on the steep eastern slope of the newly formed mountain exposed the layers of Steens Basalt and underlying formations; the surface of the block is tilted gently downward toward the west. Today the west side of the mountain slopes at 3 degrees and is about 18 miles from base to crest; the average slope of the eastern scarp is 20 degrees, and it is only 3 miles from the highest point on the crest (9,733 feet) to the desert floor more than a mile below.

The crest of Steens Mountain averages 9,300 feet in elevation and is about 20 miles long. Actually, Steens Mountain is the highest portion of a series of mountains extending from near Princeton to near Fields (e.g., Riddle Mountain, Krumbo Mountain, Steens Mountain, and the low Steens or Smith Flat). Charles Hansen, who did a biological survey of Steens Mountain, suggested the name "Alvord Mountains" for the entire range or complex.

Other prominent fault-block ranges in southeastern Oregon include Winter Ridge and Hart Mountain. Nevada can boast dozens of such ranges, many rivaling Steens Mountain in grandeur.

Steens Mountain is outlined by faults along all sides. A block of the earth's crust depressed between two faults (one on either side) is called a graben. The southern Catlow Valley is a graben between the low Steens to the east and Beatys Butte to the southwest, and the top layer of Steens Basalt underlies the floor of the valley. An uplifted block between bordering faults (e.g., Steens Mountain) is called a horst.

Mountain ranges protruding above the surrounding landscape, particularly those oriented north-south, intercept air masses, causing them to rise, cool, and release moisture. Fault-block ranges in the Great Basin receive considerably more precipitation, especially in the form of snow, than do lower areas. During the Pleistocene, for reasons that are not certain, the earth's climate cooled and an ice age of about 3 million years duration followed.

Enormous continental glaciers formed on most of the continents, and large amounts of snow and ice accumulated on higher western mountains.

After Steens Mountain was formed by uplift, streams began to erode the surface and cut deep valleys. Later, during the Pleistocene, when snow and ice accumulated to a thickness of 200 to 300 feet, the accumulation began to flow downhill as a glacier. On the general mountain surface, sheet glaciers simply moved downslope, but where streams had formed ravines or V-shaped valleys, alpine or valley glaciers followed these pre-existing pathways and transformed them into typical U-shaped valleys. Snow added near the origin of the valley glaciers sustained flow down to a point where evaporation and melting prevented further progress.

On Steens Mountain, three glacial periods and interglacial intervals have been recognized, although many more periods are evident elsewhere in North America. During the first glacial period, the mountain was covered by an extensive sheet of ice. Exposed rocks above 7,000 feet clearly show polished and scratched surfaces resulting from ice action. In the second period, glaciers were restricted to valleys, including Kiger, McCoy, Little Blitzen, Big Indian, Little Indian, and Wildhorse canyons. Fish, Mud, Bridge, and Krumbo creeks were weakly glaciated, and glaciers moved down canyons on the east scarp of the mountain to about the 6,000 foot level. During the most recent glacial period, small glaciers formed but were confined to amphitheaters or cirques at the heads of valleys.

Alpine glaciers produce a distinctive topography. A glacier erodes by plucking materials from the substrate and by abrasion, and deposits accumulated debris in terminal and lateral moraines at the point of dissipation. Tributary glaciers erode less rapidly than main valley glaciers, thus side valleys are commonly left elevated above the main valley in the form of hanging valleys, often identified by a waterfall cascading down the wall of the main valley.

A cirque is a large amphitheater at the head of a glaciated valley. Cirques have high, steep walls and often contain a lake or tarn, of which Wildhorse Lake on Steens Mountain is an example. Cirques on opposite sides of a ridge may cut through to join, thus forming a gap in the contour of the ridge called a col. Big Nick is a conspicuous col on the eastern wall of Kiger Gorge. A sharp, ragged, knife-like ridge formed between two adjacent glaciers, such as the ridge between Wildhorse and Little Alvord canyons, is called an arête.

Steens Mountain, Gearhart Mountain (south of Summer Lake),

and perhaps Drake Peak are the only glaciated fault-block ranges in southeastern Oregon. Alpine glaciers were present on half a dozen of the higher ranges farther south in the Great Basin.

During glacial periods, the elevation of permanent snowfields was as much as 3,000 feet lower than now. Because of the vast stores of water on land in the form of glaciers and accumulations of ice and snow, sea levels were at least 275 feet below those of today. In the Great Basin, glaciers and snowfields diminished during interglacial periods. The last great melt off began about 15,000 years ago and culminated about 10,000 years ago in the removal of excess snow and ice that had accumulated at higher elevations.

Times of glacial advance were also times of increased precipitation throughout the Great Basin, and as a result of increased precipitation and increased runoff, vast freshwater or pluvial lakes formed in bolsons throughout the Great Basin.

The largest of these pluvial lakes, Lake Bonneville, covered some 19,940 square miles, mostly in northwestern Utah, but also in parts of southern Idaho and eastern Nevada. Today the Great Salt Lake, which is 50 miles wide and 75 miles long, is all that remains of Lake Bonneville. Evaporation has concentrated the lake's salts to the point that only the Dead Sea, among landlocked bodies of water, has a higher salt content—and then only slightly so.

A second large pluvial lake, Lake Lahontan, sprawled over about 8,665 square miles of northwestern Nevada, portions of northeastern California, and small sections of southern Oregon. Lahontan was irregularly shaped, with many arms extending out among fault-block ranges (some mountains were reduced to mere islands). Pyramid Lake, the most notable remnant of Lake Lahontan, currently fills about 2% of Lahontan's original basin. Walker Lake is another vestige of Lake Lahontan.

In Oregon numerous small remnants of pluvial lakes still survive, including Upper Klamath, Silver, Summer, Abert, Goose, and the Warner Valley lakes. Summer and Abert lakes were once joined to form a more extensive body of water called Lake Chewaucan. Around the base of Steens Mountain, major pluvial lakes formed in the Alvord Basin (491 square miles, 200 feet deep), Catlow Valley (351 square miles, 75 feet deep), and in the Harney Basin (920 square miles, 70 feet deep), where Malheur and Harney lakes are remnants. Upper Klamath Lake has gained outlet to the sea by way of the Klamath River. Catlow Lake, which at one time was one of the larger bodies of water in southeastern Oregon, is now totally dry.

In most instances former shorelines of these ancient lakes are

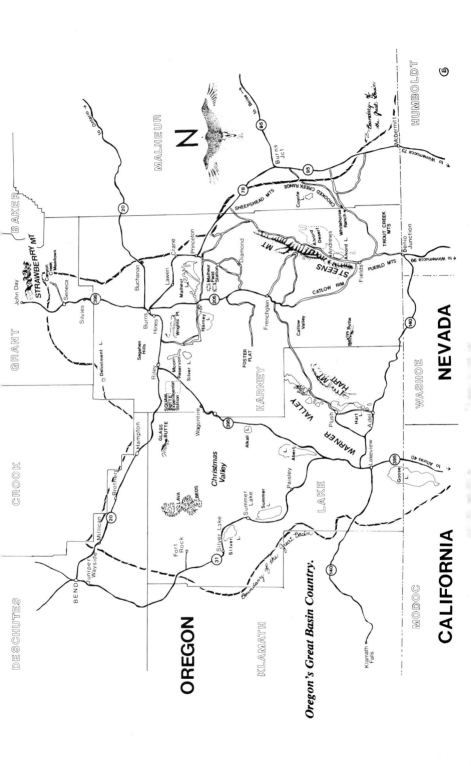

Oregon's Great Basin Country.

Visitors will find a bit of the old west in Frenchglen and other basin hamlets.

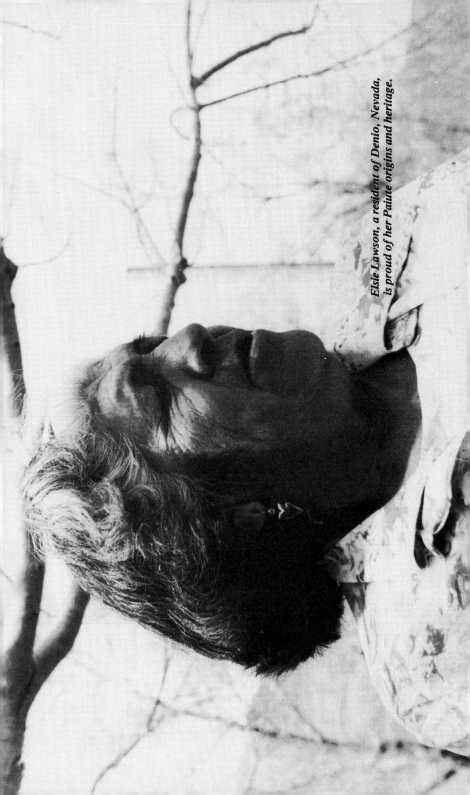

Elsie Lawson, a resident of Denio, Nevada, is proud of her Paiute origins and heritage.

Peter French built this willow corral and barn at the P Ranch — Malheur Refuge has restored them.

clearly visible as terraces standing 70 to 300 feet above current water levels. In many basins extensive salt deposits are all that remain; the water has long since seeped into the earth or evaporated.

After the great lava flows and episodes of fault-block mountain building, local volcanism and limited faulting continued to alter the landscape, but in recent times, spectacular changes have resulted from erosion and deposition.

Glaciers gouged out U-shaped valleys and transported gigantic boulders and huge amounts of other debris towards the mouths of canyons. Torrents from glacial melt swept other materials, including moraines abandoned by retreating glaciers, down into basins and built alluvial fans. Along the Steens Mountain scarp some fans extend as much as 2 miles out onto the desert floor beyond their canyons. Eventually basins were literally buried in alluvium, the finer material being transported farthest from original sources. Because glacial sediment is a loosely packed assortment of various materials, many streams, especially during periods of low flow, emerge from canyons only to disappear into their own fans or other accumulated alluvium on the desert floor. Episodic mudflows, triggered by unusual amounts of runoff, continue to build alluvial fans.

Sheet and gully erosion effectively degrade exposed desert landscapes where sparse vegetation provides minimal protection. Steeper terrain, such as a fault scarp, is particularly vulnerable to erosion by landslides as well. During wet periods, water laden with fine sand, silt, clay, and dissolved salts accumulates in playas. The water eventually evaporates leaving the solids and salts on the surface. The Alvord Desert east of Steens Mountain is such an alkali flat, and there are thousands of others in the Great Basin.

Although wind erodes all land surfaces to some extent, it is a particularly effective erosional agent in arid regions where flat terrain, dry surfaces, unconsolidated bedrock, and sparse vegetative cover exist. Seasonal standing water and excessive salinity prevent vegetation from growing on many playas, making them prime areas for wind erosion. Predominantly westerly and southwesterly winds remove fine materials from playa surfaces and build sand dunes along the lee fringes of the playa. During periods of strong winds, this phenomenon may produce violent dust storms downwind from large playas such as Harney Lake.

Throughout the Great Basin, wind has swept fine material from basins and deposited it, usually along eastern margins of basins. Removal of fine materal may leave a desert pavement in which adjacent pebbles and rocks form a mosaic resembling a terrazzo-like surface. In many localities the exposed rocks in desert

9

pavement are coated with a brownish or blackish shiny crust—aptly called desert varnish. Desert varnish is composed of fine clay particles (probably wind transported) bound by iron and manganese oxides from surface and capillary sources of water.

Because of the great amount of exposed rock and extreme fluctuations in temperatures, ice fracturing, caused by the alternate freezing and thawing of water enclosed in cracks and crevices, is also an important degradational process in the high desert.

The current landscape of the northern Great Basin reflects regional geological events, as well as episodes of local geological significance. The pluvial lake formed in the Harney Basin found outlet to the sea by draining eastward near Princeton into the South Fork of the Malheur River. When lava flows blocked this channel near Malheur Cave, overflow escaped from a second outlet near Crane Gap. Because of these outlets, water depth in the Harney Basin probably did not exceed 70 feet. Under the influence of a warmer and drier climate, the large lake receded to its modern remnants—Malheur and Harney lakes. Presently Malheur Lake is fed by local springs, the Silvies River draining the south slope of the Blue Mountains, and the Blitzen or Donner und Blitzen River draining the west slope of Steens Mountain. Between 1825 and 1850, Malheur Lake probably dried up periodically, and in 1934 it was completely dry, but refilled when years of adequate rainfall followed. Silver Creek, which drains highlands northwest of Burns, several large springs, and periodic overflow from Malheur Lake feed Harney Lake, which dries up each summer. Few streams in the northern Great Basin really deserve to be called rivers.

Springs, many of them hot, are scattered throughout the Great Basin, especially along fault zones. Some larger springs, such as Sod House Spring near headquarters of the Malheur National Wildlife Refuge, may discharge over 18 cubic feet of water per second. In Oregon, hot springs occur near Crane, on the south margin of Harney Lake, at Mickey Hot Springs and Borax Lake in the Alvord Basin, on Hart Mountain, and in numerous other localities. Northern Nevada has many hot springs. Some springs range up to 200°F, while others such as Mickey Hot Springs are modified as steam vents or boiling mud pots. Springs offering moderate temperatures have been favorite bathing sites for generations of desert travelers.

North of Lakeview are numerous hot springs. Certain wells drilled in this area erupt in geyser fashion. Hunter's Hot Spring erupts at about 30-second intervals, spurting water a few feet to 40 or 50 feet into the air. Crump Geyser, another drilled well, erupts violently at about 80-minute intervals.

Alluvial deposits in bolsons vary greatly in thickness. In the Harney Basin, alluvium thickness is generally less than 300 feet, while Death Valley contains about 10,000 feet of fill. Lowland soils range from thick, well drained, and fertile soils to thin and strongly alkaline soils with a well developed hardpan. Most upland soils are shallow with silica-lime hardpans. Many desert soils in the northern Great Basin contain considerable unconsolidated volcanic material.

Travelers in the great interior basins of southeastern Oregon are humbled by the imposing horizons. Rims, cliffs, buttes, mesas, and monumental talus slopes form precipitous boundaries between basins and surrounding highland plateaus. Although the stark images of arid topography may suggest a violent past, desert landscapes provide the naturalist and photographer with immeasurable delights.

CHAPTER 3

Climate and Weather

In Chapter 2 we learned that lowlands in the northern Great Basin experienced a mild, comparatively moist climate before being cut off from marine sources of moisture by intervening mountain ranges. Also, the effects of drastic climatic changes accompanying glacial and pluvial periods were described. Now it is time to examine the diverse conditions responsible for the region's modern climate and day to day weather.

Much insight into the prevailing climate can be gained by studying climatic events at selected points along a transect drawn from the Pacific Coast of Oregon to the interior valleys of the northern Great Basin. Because few weather stations record complete weather data and stations are seldom found in sparsely populated, non-agricultural areas, a "transect" including the desired geographical features cannot be a straight line (Table 1).

Air masses moving or lingering over the ocean for reasonably long periods of time gain moisture through evaporation and gradually acquire temperatures approaching those of the surface water. In winter, the Pacific Ocean along the coast is relatively warmer than the adjacent land, therefore maritime air masses coming ashore are typically warm and humid. Warm air will hold more water vapor than cold air—an increase of 18°F nearly doubles the moisture-holding capacity of air. Because warm air is lighter and tends to rise, these air masses are usually associated with areas of low air pressure.

When prevailing westerly winds bring these maritime air masses ashore, heat exchange causes the land to be warmed and the air masses to be cooled. If the cooling air reaches the dew point (i.e., the temperature at which a mass of air becomes saturated and water vapor condenses as a liquid or solid), water vapor condenses and precipitation forms.

In the summertime, ocean surfaces and maritime air masses are relatively colder than adjacent coastal lands. Onshore winds are composed of relatively cool, dry, and dense air, which is usually associated with high air pressures. Over the land, the air warms, expands, and becomes drier as its water-holding capacity increases. This process can be observed when offshore fog disappears after being driven a short distance inland; visible water droplets are transformed into invisible water vapor—the reverse of condensation. In the summer, marine air cools the coastal zone, and the high pressure associated with these air masses prevents "lows" from approaching the shore. Summer "highs" blocking out "lows" produces extended periods of fair weather along the coast.

Coastal winds tend to blow from the northwest in the summer and from the southwest in the winter. Winter warming and summer cooling of the Oregon coast is accentuated by the Aleutian Current. July average temperature at Newport is only 13°F above the January average; the difference is 44°F at Andrews in the Great Basin (Table 1). Furthermore, the difference between record low and high temperatures is only 99° at Newport, compared with 140° at Andrews.

Table 1. Climatic data for selected stations from Newport on the Oregon coast to Andrews, east of Steens Mountain in the Great Basin. Elevation is given in feet, precipitation in inches, temperature in degrees F, and growing season in days—all rounded to the nearest whole number. Data from *Climate and Man* (see Selected Readings and References).

	Newport	Glenora	Corvallis	Govt. Camp	Bend	Burns	Andrews
Elevation	134	1500	224	3980	3623	4148	4146
Precipitation	66	129	40	85	13	12	7
July Ave. Temp.	57	63	66	56	65	67	73
Jan. Ave. Temp.	44	37	39	30	31	25	29
Record Low Temp.	1	3	-14	-16	-26	-32	-33
Record High Temp.	100	106	106	96	105	102	107
Growing Season	248	140	191	<80	91	117	147

As air masses move inland, they are forced up the western slope of the Coast Range, which is 1,000 to 2,000 feet high in most places. Temperatures are lower at higher elevations, the decrease amounting to about 3.6°F for each 1,000 feet. But air moving up a slope becomes less dense as air pressure decreases. Because molecules of air collide less frequently, rising air cools at a rate of about 5.5°F per 1,000 feet. If air cools to the dew point and precipitation forms, heavy rains may occur, especially during the winter (e.g., 129 inches per year at Glenora). When water vapor condenses, heat is released, and the air warms and tends to rise—thus, cooling may reoccur and additional precipitation may form. Precipitation produced from cooling air masses being forced over mountains is called orographic precipitation. Clouds forming over mountains, as water vapor condenses into visible droplets, often suggest impending orographic precipitation.

Air masses descending the eastern slope of the Coast Range are warmed (i.e., lower elevation and increased pressure), gain water-holding capacity, and produce less precipitation (only 40 inches at Corvallis vs. 129 at Glenora). A zone of decreased rainfall on the lee side of a mountain is called a rain shadow—thus, the Willamette Valley lies in the rain shadow of the Coast Range (inhabitants of the Willamette Valley may find this hard to believe).

Masses of air moving up and over the Cascade Mountains (average height 5,000 feet, with some peaks above 10,000 feet) are again subjected to orographic influences and may again be forced to relinquish precipitation, often in the form of snow (the annual precipitation of 85 inches at Government Camp includes more than 100 inches of snowfall). Descending air along the eastern front of the Cascade Range forms a rain shadow, and Bend gets only 13 inches of annual precipitation. The Cascades further diminish the moderating influences of the Pacific Ocean, permitting temperatures to be more extreme east of the crest (Table 1).

In the vicinity of Bend and eastward through the Great Basin, a marked reduction in cloud cover, generally higher elevations, and clear, dry air favor maximum solar radiation (i.e., sunshine). Temperatures of soil surfaces and air near the ground are high during summer days. The same conditions responsible for high daytime temperatures facilitate reradiation and loss of heat to the atmosphere and outer space at night. Rapid cooling after sunset and extremely cold winter nights characterize the interior highlands. The effect is even more apparent at Burns than at Bend.

Air masses reaching Steens Mountain are quite dry, having lost much moisture along the way, but may once more be relieved of moisture as they are forced up and over the range. Andrews, with about seven inches of precipitation a year, is in the rain shadow of Steens Mountain and has the distinction of being the driest weather station in Oregon.

Climatic events along the transect (Table 1) can be summarized as follows: annual precipitation decreases on the lee side of each mountain range, and seasonal and daily temperature extremes increase with distance from the ocean. Growing season, the summer frost-free period, generally decreases inland, but is strongly influenced by local topography. Actually, all the factors are subject to a certain amount of local variation, but the transect clearly reveals the enormous effects of mountain barriers upon the climate of the Great Basin.

Relative humidity is the amount of moisture in the air compared to the amount it could hold if saturated (expressed as a percentage) at a given temperature. Low relative humidities in the Great Basin reflect orographic influences and are accentuated by generally high summer temperatures. Dry air, which enhances evaporation of perspiration in the summer and diminishes cold chill in the winter, makes desert temperature extremes more tolerable to people, but may severely stress desert plants and animals. Annual evapotranspiration (i.e., evaporation plus water losses from plant surfaces) from Malheur Lake amounts to about 40 inches, even though annual precipitation barely exceeds 8 inches. Because of such dry air, precipitation falling from clouds over the desert will often evaporate at lower altitudes before reaching the ground. Heavy rains often produce puddles and fail to penetrate bare desert soils, consequently much incoming moisture is lost through evaporation, especially when winds are strong.

In the winter, owing to the greater tilt of the northern hemisphere away from the sun, solar radiation is less direct in the northern hemisphere, and general cooling occurs. In summer, incoming radiation strikes the earth at angles approaching 90 degrees and heats the surface more efficiently. Generally, areas of low pressure build over heated surfaces as air warms, expands, and rises; "highs" tend to form over cooler surfaces. In the winter, "lows" originate in the North Pacific in the vicinity of the Subpolar Front and develop further as they move down across the ocean and come inland, usually over British Columbia, Washington, and Oregon. Extremely cold masses of air form continental highs in the Canadian Arctic and move southward through the central United States. When continental highs are shunted west of the Rocky Mountains and down into the Great Basin, and when sufficiently strong, the "high" may divert incoming maritime "lows", producing unusually cold, clear

15

weather—often lasting several days or even weeks.

Precipitation may occur along points of contact (fronts) between warm and cool air masses. Movement of various frontal systems may be modified by jet streams, topography (particularly in mountainous regions), and other factors.

In the summer, the activity zone for maritime "lows" shifts northward, as does the more southerly zone of subtropical "highs". When strong subtropical highs move inland from over the Pacific, usually into southern California, they may generate extremely hot, dry winds called Santa Ana Winds. "Santa anas" are often violent and may cause widespread damage. Also, pressure differences between fronts often produce forceful winds in the northern Great Basin, When a strong "high" is located west of the Cascade Mountains and a "low" is on the east side, strong, dry winds blow eastward across the mountains, warming and drying as they descend. These warm winds, called foehns or chinooks, may melt and evaporate several inches of snow in a few hours, leaving the ground dusty dry.

High surface temperatures and ascending, turbulent air favor the formation of dust devils, especially over playas and other flatlands. On extremely hot days, violent updrafts of hot air may carry large quantities of dust aloft, producing dust clouds and dust storms.

If heated air rises sufficiently, it may produce condensation, form massive piles of thunderhead clouds, and develop into a convection storm. Convection storms may grow into thunderstorms, accompanied by lightning and thunder. Lightning is an electrical discharge compensating for differences in electrical potential between clouds, parts of a cloud, or a cloud and the ground. As lightning travels along a path, it burns part of the atmospheric oxygen, creating a partial vacuum. Air rushing immediately into the partial vacuum collides to produce the sound of thunder. Thunderstorms are fairly numerous in the northern Great Basin (averaging 10 per year at Winnemucca), and may produce more rainfall in a few minutes than would be normal in several months. Severe cloudbursts occasionally result in devastating torrents of water when runoff is funneled through narrow canyons—the danger being extreme in some areas in the southern Great Basin. Large amounts of debris may be transported by floods and debris flows produced by cloudbursts.

In canyons and to a lesser extent on mountain slopes, updrafts of rising warm air may produce persistent uphill winds during the day. After sunset cold air drainage begins as the ground surface cools, and cool winds drain downward, especially through canyons.

Occasionally local topography strongly modifies local weather. Abundant snowfall at higher elevations stores potential irrigation water that is essential to agricultural endeavors in adjacent lowlands. Temperature inversions in closed basins may trap and hold smoke or other noxious substances in stagnant air, causing serious episodes of air pollution. Salt Lake City is vulnerable to such episodes. Minor topographical features may strongly influence local weather patterns. Wright's Point, south of Burns, Oregon, frequently disrupts storms so that rain or snow falls on one side but not the other.

In the Great Basin, summer skies are often cloudless or populated with scattered cumulus clouds. Other cloud types are less common, transitory, and generally associated with weather changes or storm systems. The depth of air traversed by light, air density, and scattering caused by particles in the atmosphere determine sky color. When the sun is directly overhead, the scattering of blue wavelengths gives the sky its blue color. At dawn and sunset, light passing through a greater depth of atmosphere scatters red wavelengths and produces spectacular desert sunsets.

Great variation characterizes the weather and climate of the northern Great Basin. The differences between mean daily high and low temperatures is about 37°F at several localities in the northern Great Basin. Seasonal differences in temperature and precipitation are usually large. Annual variation can be huge (e.g., Burns received less than 6 inches of precipitation in 1937 and almost 17 inches in 1940). Tree ring analyses and recorded measurements show long periods of drastic climatic variation (e.g., Malheur Lake was dry in 1934 but covered 67,000 acres in 1952). The difference between pluvial times and today attests to even longer climatic cycles.

Before judging the weather and climate of the northern Great Basin too harshly, one should look elsewhere. In Death Valley, farther south, the temperature exceeds 120°F at least once a month from May to October. In 1959 the temperature exceeded 100° every day except one between May 30 and September 12, and in 1913 it remained 120° and above for two weeks. The highest air temperature recorded in Death Valley is 134°—the record ground temperature is 190°. At Furnace Creek annual precipitation averages 1.5 inches, and as much as 15 months has passed without a measurable trace of precipitation. Only twice in 50 years has the annual amount exceeded 4 inches. Perhaps the northern Great Basin isn't so bad after all.

CHAPTER 4

History

Human culture in the northern Great Basin dates back to the times of pluvial lakes, perhaps as long as 11,000 years ago. Sage-bark sandals discovered in Fort Rock Cave and dated by radiocarbon at about 9,000 years of age provide the first evidence of human habitation in the region. Much mystery surrounds these early people, their origins, descendants, and ways of life. Simple obsidian artifacts and undeciphered pictographs and petroglyphs provide scant legacy of a people who may have witnessed the eruption of Mount Mazama (to form Crater Lake) about 6,600 years ago, shared a landscape with the last of the great Pleistocene mammals, and experienced the drastic climatic changes that transformed pluvial lakes into dusty desert basins. Although the life style of early basin people is obscure, it probably did not differ much from the life style of Northern Paiute Indians who lived in the area when white men arrived.

Bands of Northern Paiutes were known to each other by dietary resources available in each locality. There were nearly two dozen such bands with names like Groundhog Eaters (Warner Valley and adjacent parts of northern Nevada and California), Pine-nut Eaters (near Paisley, Oregon), Wada (a plant) Eaters (Harney Basin), Berry Eaters (Alvord Basin), Jackrabbit Eaters (north of Pyramid Lake), Cui-ui (a fish) Eaters (around Pyramid and Winnemucca lakes), and others. In reality, these names are useful but misleading, for Paiutes were characterized by an uncanny ability to exploit all available food resources. They ate almost every potential food except coyotes, magpies, and other carrion eaters.

Paiutes had no tribes or other complex social organizations. The basic unit was the family consisting of the man, wife or wives (sisters commonly married the same man), children, perhaps one or both grandparents, sometimes an aunt or uncle, or others. On occasions, several family groups came together to cooperate in game drives, to exploit attractive food sources, or for festivals. Peter Skeene Ogden expressed amazement at the number of Indians he encountered near Malheur Lake. But large permanent assemblages would have exhausted local food and fuel supplies, and the usual density for Northern Paiute people could only be described as sparse—perhaps one family per 100 square miles.

Although not really nomadic, Northern Paiutes moved regularly with the seasonal availability of various food supplies. Life consisted of continual, systematic migrations in search of food, firewood, water, materials for shelter, tools, and clothing. The Indians had little regard for material things, which was in keeping with their great mobility. Although feral horses were present, unlike Indians in some other parts of the West who used them as early as 1750, the Paiutes walked and probably used horses only for food, at least until white men came. When food or fuel became scarce at a particular camp site, extra tools, heavy grindstones, and excess food stores were cached for future use, while waterjugs, babies in cradleboards, and other essential belongings were gathered and moved to a new camp. Great distances were traveled during the annual cycle to harvest seeds, berries, fish, and game.

In the early spring, ground squirrels emerging from hibernation were trapped, snared, or shot with bow and arrow. Waterfowl captured in nets woven of plant fibers were placed on open coals and eagerly devoured after the charred feathers and skin had been peeled away. Ducks not needed immediately were split and dried for later use. New shoots and roots of bulrushes, cattails, and other marsh plants were relished after long winters without green foods and were often eaten on the spot. Rafts or boats prepared of bundles of bulrush stems bound together with cordage were used to collect waterfowl eggs. Disposable baskets of cattail or bulrush leaves were used to transport the eggs, including partially incubated eggs which were not rejected. Camas, wild carrot, bitterroot, and wild onions were dug with pointed sticks, eaten fresh, cooked in rock ovens in the ground, or dried for winter use.

Using baskets, nets, harpoons, traps, or quick hands, Paiutes took fish whenever water was free of ice, but spawning runs attracted eager crowds from afar. When Tahoe suckers (Cui-ui) ascended the Truckee River from Pyramid and Winnemucca lakes and when the great Lahontan cutthroats ascended the Walker River from Walker Lake, excitement and festivity reached a fevered pitch. The Indians gorged themselves and smoked or dried the surplus.

In the summer, pollen from cattails and many kinds of seeds, such as desert sunflower and Indian ricegrass, were gathered. Seeds were shaken or threshed into baskets and winnowed. Bunches of nearly ripened vegetation were placed on coals and the roasted seeds winnowed from the ashes. Seeds were often ground, cooked into a gruel, and eaten with the fingers. Family groups participated in organized drives for coots or flightless waterfowl in molt. Serviceberries, chokecherries, and other fruit were sauced, made into cakes, and dried.

In the fall, Paiutes journeyed to basin mountain ranges supporting Piñon pine and gathered the seeds or nuts. Large caches were set aside for winter use. Tubers were dug and dried. Also, fall was the season for large organized rabbit drives. Nets of nettles, milkweed, or wild hemp cordage, usually about 3 feet tall and sometimes hundreds of feet long, were set in suitable habitat. Lines of young men drove the rabbits into the nets, and the older men clubbed the rabbits and reset the nets. The entire rabbit was used—meat, bones, and especially the skins, which were woven into the Indian's prized and most essential possession, the rabbit-skin blanket.

Large amounts of food had to be prepared and stored for winter, when hunting was less productive. Also, fiber and other materials were collected to be woven into baskets, nets, and other useful items during long hours spent in shelters around the fire. Indians wove baskets, bowls, and waterjugs that were nearly waterproof, but a mixture of pitch and clay was added to the outside to make the containers absolutely tight. They had very little pottery; such heavy wares were impractical in a migratory life style. Cooking was done by dropping hot rocks into baskets of water and food—a pinenut mush could be quickly brought to a rolling boil.

Although Northern Paiutes made arrow points, scrapers, and various other implements from obsidian and chert and used the bow and arrow, bow hunting was much less important in food getting than we might imagine. Small game was more often captured in snares, traps, or deadfalls. Taking large game required great skill or a community effort, consequently, deer, elk, mountain sheep, and pronghorns were rarely eaten.

Paiutes were naked most of the time. Rabbit-skin blankets containing several dozens of rabbit skins served as bed, blanket, and clothes when worn as a hooded shawl. Sandals of sagebrush bark were worn. Because skins of large animals were seldom available and because Paiutes did not know how to waterproof tanned hides, moccasins were practically unknown. Tanned leather was more likely to be used for pouches to carry valuables and small decorative items. In extremely cold weather, sagebrush bark leggings might be worn. Women occasionally wore skirts of sagebrush bark and wore bowl-shaped basketry caps atop their heads. The thong was valued as a device for carrying bows, game, and other items.

Shelters of various types were fashioned of local materials for warmth or shade. Boughs, limbs, and other vegetation placed on poles suspended between shrubs formed a lean-to. Mats of woven cattail or other vegetation were attached to willow frames to form huts resembling an inverted bowl. A hole was left for smoke to exit. Occasionally these crude structures were reinforced and repaired for occupancy in subsequent years. Caves were used as shelter. Paiutes did not use conventional tepees.

Gossiping, gambling, storytelling, dancing, singing, and games were favorite pastimes, especially during fall and winter group encampments. Trading with other groups of Indians was probably limited and confined to food items, shell, and other materials not locally available. Religion was not organized, but Paiutes had a highly personal reverence for spirits thought to dwell in coyotes, petroglyphs, and various natural phenomena. Special rites, celebrations, and taboos associated with birth, puberty, and death were commonly observed by Northern Paiute people.

When white men first entered the Great Basin, many died of starvation, thirst, and exposure in the lands where Indians had survived for centuries. Although Indians posed a threat to the first travelers and homesteaders, settler communities grew and the white people became more secure. Fences appeared; cattle and sheep moved into ranges formerly belonging to the Paiutes. Naturally the Indians objected to the intrusion into their homelands and the destruction of their food resources. Some of the Northern Paiutes joined the Bannocks in a futile uprising in 1878. The defeated and disorganized Paiutes were exiled to the Yakima Reservation in Washington, where many died, while whites moved onto their reservation lands. Ultimately the Indians returned home to nothing. Unable to resume their old ways, they attempted to survive on the fringe of white man's society as their former skills were forgotten. Today, a proud, industrious people have been reduced to a life of servitude, welfare, and poverty in obscure corners of lands that were once theirs.

Perhaps the first white men to see the high desert lands of the northwestern Great Basin were three Frenchmen, Charbonneau, La Valle, and Nadeau, who left their ship near San Diego in about 1750 and set out overland for Quebec. Two of these men are known to have reached southern Idaho where they settled and lived with Indians.

In 1825 Peter Skeene Ogden, chief trader for the Hudson Bay Company and a legendary figure in the early West, with about 100 men set out from Fort Nez Perce (Walla Walla) to trap beaver and explore along the Snake River and its tributaries. Near the mouth of the Malheur River, Antoine Sylvaille with five men was dispatched to trap and explore the Malheur. Early in 1826 the small group reached a river which Ogden was to name the Sylvaille River—later shortened to Silvies. The Sylvaille party was apparently the first group of white men to enter the Harney Basin. When robbed of furs and other valuables by Indians, Sylvaille's party selected the French adjective *malheur*, meaning unfortunate, as a name for the Malheur River. Later, the name was also given to Malheur Lake because of an erroneous notion that the lake drained into a tributary of the Malheur River (actually it did during or after the Pleistocene!).

In the fall of 1826, Ogden and 35 men returned to the Harney Basin and discovered Malheur, Mud, and Harney lakes, which were labeled the Youxpell Lakes on a map of 1833 prepared in England. Food was scarce, so the group resorted to eating bear and beaver when deer and pronghorns eluded them. Ogden returned to the basin in 1827 and was able to trap 150 prime beaver in only 3 weeks. On his way back from a trip to the headwaters of the Humboldt River in 1828-29, Ogden once again passed through the Harney Basin.

John Work, also a chief trader for the Hudson Bay Company, traveled along the east side of Steens Mountain in 1831 and named it Snow Mountain. The current name honors Major Enoch Steen, who crossed the mountain in pursuit of Indians in 1860. Later, Work turned north to Harney Lake, which was known as Sylvailles Lake at the time. It seems unfortunate that the barrage of names proposed by early explorers has persisted at the expense of original Paiute names.

In 1843 John C. Fremont and a government-sponsored party of explorers with the celebrated Kit Carson as guide, passed through central Oregon, naming Summer Lake, Winter Ridge, and Abert Lake (which John Work had called Salt Lake in 1832). Fremont continued into the Great Basin, a name he proposed, searching for the non-existent Buenaventure River, which reputedly flowed from a vast salt lake to the Pacific Ocean. Fremont's glowing accounts of his explorations earned him the title of The Pathfinder. But his misleading description of the Humboldt River Valley is credited with causing great hardship among immigrants, who arrived expecting to find a lush landscape rather than a narrow channel winding through hostile desert. Pierson Reading and a small group bound for California crossed the Harney Basin in 1843 on the strength of Fremont's account. He later wrote a vivid description of the terrain and the party's hardships, such as being without water for 30 hours.

Before 1843 the westward migration involved small, loosely organized groups, but in that year, the first great wagon train of more than 1,000 people came west, triggering a veritable stampede in succeeding years. Fort Hall in Idaho became a major separation point, where traffic destined for California turned southward from the Oregon contingent. The Oregon Trail ran north of the Great Basin, passing over the Blue Mountains and down to the Columbia River. In August of 1845, when an Oregon-bound caravan reached the vicinity of Ontario, Stephen Hall Meek, who claimed to have traveled through the Harney Basin in 1835, persuaded part of the wagon train to turn south of the Blue Mountains along a route that was later to be known as the Meek Cutoff. Meek argued that leaving the Oregon Trail at that point would save time and distance. He offered to lead the way for $5.00 per wagon. About 800 people, owning 200 wagons and several thousand head of assorted livestock, accepted Meek's offer and set off into the high desert during the hottest month of the year.

The wagon train encountered no more than the usual adversities until they crossed the Silvies River. But near Harney Lake, drinkable water could not be found, so the group was forced to travel more than 35 miles west through difficult and desolate terrain before finding springs at Wagontire Peak. Scouting farther west revealed no other water, and it became obvious that the wagon train was hopelessly lost. Forage and provisions were in short supply. As anger flared to open revolt, Meek departed in fear of his life. He eventually reached The Dalles and returned with a rescue party. Meanwhile the wagon train split up into small wandering groups, each hoping to find a way out of their terrible predicament. Livestock died or was abandoned, personal belongings were jettisoned to lighten the loads, and 75 persons lost their lives before the "Lost Wagon Train" finally reached The Dalles. The portion of the train that stayed on the Oregon Trail had long since reached the Willamette Valley.

Along the route taken by Meek's wagon train, a member of the party collected some souvenir rocks and placed them in a blue bucket. Perhaps because of the distractions of great adversity, the rocks were forgotten, but when eventually examined, were found to contain large amounts of pure gold. Legions of treasure hunters have attempted to retrace the erratic route of the Lost Wagon Train, but the famous Blue Bucket Mine has eluded discovery. Had the gold actually been discovered in 1845, it would have preceded discovery at Sutter's Mill by 3 years and would have profoundly changed the subsequent history and patterns of settlement in the West.

In ensuing years, a few other wagon trains took the Meek Cutoff, but most endured hardship and regretted their choice. In 1853 a caravan ran out of food and had no flour for a month. The people survived by eating insects, horses, and what could be scavenged from the desert. A rescue party sent from the Willamette Valley prevented a total disaster.

In 1859 Captain Henry Wallace brought U.S. troops into the Harney Basin seeking an improved route to Salt Lake City. He renamed Sylvailles Lake for Brigadier General W.J. Harney. Another surveying detachment brought to the area in 1860 by Captain Andrew Smith engaged in battle with 150 Indians. Major Enoch Steen, who was examining possible routes for roads over the Cascades, received news of Smith's encounter and brought his troops to the rescue. Smith and Steen remained in the area, surveying, naming various landmarks, and preparing improved maps.

Traffic in the northern Great Basin increased remarkably in the early 1860's when gold was discovered in Baker County, Oregon (1861), where the town of Auburn rapidly grew to 6,000 people, surpassing Portland in population. The next year gold was found at Whiskey Gulch (Grant County, Oregon). Some estimates claim that as many as 10,000 persons were drawn there by the promise of glitter. Eventually $26,000,000 worth of gold was extracted near Canyon City. The famous Idaho City gold find also occurred in 1862. In 1863 gold (and later silver) was found near Silver City in southwestern Idaho. Other strikes followed in British Columbia, northern Idaho, and Montana. Hordes of fortune seekers, primarily from Nevada and California, frantically rushed from strike to strike. Empty desert byways became clogged with miners, pack trains, and all manner of travel.

In 1862, two sets of brothers named Chapman and Stenger came to the Harney Basin to trap. They built the first permanent residence, a sod house, near the current location of the headquarters of Malheur National Wildlife Refuge. The nearby community still bears the "Sod House" name.

As Western military units were drawn into the Civil War, Indians enjoyed greater freedom and became increasingly bold during the early 1860's. After the war, a growing white population demanded protection, and a series of army camps was established for that purpose—Camp Steele (14 miles east of Burns; renamed Fort Harney in 1867), Camp Lyon (on the Owyhee River near the Oregon-Idaho border; later called Camp Three Forks), Camp Alvord (near Andrews at the eastern base of Steens Mountain), Camp C.F. Smith (on Whitehorse Creek north of Quinn River Mountain), Camp Bidwell (in northeastern California near the Nevada border), Camp Wright (at the east end of Wright's Point), and Camp Currey (on Silver Creek, 45 miles west of Fort Harney). Camp Currey was named for Colonel George B. Currey, who named the Donner und Blitzen River (German for thunder and lightning), which had previously been called the New River. Other camps were established in adjoining areas. By 1868, the Indians were largely under control, and the lush interior valleys began to look more and more attractive to white men seeking land.

In the summer of 1869, John S. Devine, the first of the cattle barons and the first permanent settler in Oregon's Great Basin country, arrived to claim lands abandoned at the site of the sprawling military camp, C.F. Smith. No other permanent settlers were within 200 miles, and Indians prowled the land. Devine came from California with the financial backing of W.B. Todhunter, a wealthy Sacramento butcher. Devine, who was 30 years old, arrived ready to build a livestock empire, bringing nearly 3,000 head of cattle, a large herd of horses, half a dozen vaqueros, a cook, and supply wagon. In his customary dress of a Spanish don and mounted astride a magnificent white horse adorned with silver trappings, Devine was a frontier aristocrat. His Whitehorse Ranch became widely known for its hospitality and charm—a microcosm of fine race horses, fine wines, and exquisite foods in a vast rugged land otherwise devoid of such refinements. Devine's holdings expanded to include much of the land along the east side of Steens Mountain, where he developed the Alvord Ranch. Devine purchased large parcels of "swampland" from the state for $1.25 per acre with 20% down.

Today the Alvord and Whitehorse ranches remain showplaces, and the famous weather vane of a white horse stands atop Devine's barn—still in excellent condition—as a fitting reminder of the unique pioneer cattleman. Devine died in 1901 and is buried in Burns.

By 1871 several others had taken land in the Harney and Alvord basins. Then in 1872, Peter French, who was destined to become a Western legend, rode into the Blitzen Valley. French was an employee of Dr. Hugh Glenn, who controlled extensive lands in the Sacramento Valley and was the largest grower of wheat in the United States. French was made a partner with the responsibility of relocating and managing part of Glenn's cattle operations. Peter French, whose legal name was John William, was only 23 years old, weighed 135 pounds, and stood 5 feet 5 inches tall. But his physical stature concealed immense ambition, courage, and ability. After 2 months on the trail, French entered Catlow Valley with 1,200 head of cattle, more than 20 horses, wagons, supplies, a cook, and a few Mexican vaqueros and hands. Near Roaring Springs he was fortunate to meet a discouraged prospector named Porter, from whom he purchased a few cattle and the now famous P brand, which entitled him to grazing rights on most of the west side of Steens Mountain.

French located his headquarters, the picturesque P Ranch, along the Blitzen River near the base of Steens Mountain and turned his energies to the task at hand. He ditched and drained swampland, cut native hay for winter fodder, built quality fences and corrals, and constructed magnificent barns, while continually improving his herds and acquiring new land. Within 4 years he was selling cattle by driving them 200 miles to the railroad in Winnemucca. In 1878, his cattle sales brought $125,665. Eventually French's rambling spread extended from Catlow Valley to Malheur Lake, and "branch" ranches in the Blitzen Valley were opened at Buena Vista, Diamond, Riddle Ranch, Krumbo, Barton Lake, and Sod House. He also had several ranches in the Catlow Valley, the largest of which was at Roaring Springs.

In 1883 Pete entered into an ill-fated marriage with Ella Glenn, Dr. Glenn's daughter. His bride, accustomed to the opulent life of San Francisco, refused to move to Oregon. Then, 16 days after the marriage, Dr. Glenn was murdered by a discontented former employee. Glenn left a legally tangled and indebted estate. His heirs and estate administrators drained funds from French's profitable operation to pay bills. In 1891, Ella was granted an uncontested divorce with custody of their son.

As the number of settlers in the Blitzen Valley increased, French was drawn into numerous disputes over land and water rights. Fences were cut, haystacks set afire, and cattle stolen. The Glenn heirs and estate managers insisted that French deal with his neighbors harshly, which alienated many of his former friends. Peter lost significant land holdings to new settlers through litigation. Then on 26 December 1897, a recent settler, Ed Oliver, quarreled briefly with French and shot him. Oliver was arrested but released on bail. Although French was unarmed and his buckaroos had witnessed the shooting, Oliver was acquitted by a 12-man jury after only 3 hours of deliberation. The body of Pete French was taken to Baker, Oregon and shipped to California for burial.

Controversy still surrounds the name of French. He had shown great bravery in fighting hostile Indians during the Bannock War. Thanks to his foresight in storing hay, his herds survived the terrible winter of 1889, while his neighbors suffered disastrous losses. French practiced good husbandry and respected quality in a time and place where such considerations were uncommon. He came to a wilderness, built an empire of 45,000 head of cattle and 150,000 acres of land, left a lasting legacy, and lost his life—all in the short span of 25 years.

Heinrich Alfred Kreiser was born in Germany and came to San Francisco, using the borrowed name of Henry Miller, actually the name of a friend who had booked passage on the boat but had to cancel at the last moment. In 1850 when Miller, who chose to retain his new name, arrived in San Francisco at age 23 with 6 dollars in his pocket, he took work as a butcher, providing meat for the prodigious appetites of the gold miners. When Miller died at age 89 in 1916, he was the world's undisputed cattle king, owner of a million head of cattle, more than a million acres of land in five states, two banks and their branches, and numerous other properties appraised at $50,000,000. He had $10,000,000 in his bank account, owed no one, and could ride from Oregon's Silvies Valley to the Kern River in California and camp on his own land each night.

Young Miller began by working long hours in his meat business and saving his money. In 1858 he formed a partnership with Charles Lux. They purchased 1,000 head of cattle and land in the San Joaquin Valley and soon spread out in all directions, eventually acquiring ranches east of the mountains in Nevada. Lux died in 1887. After a 20-year court battle, Miller bought out the Lux heirs.

When Miller saw some prime cattle from southeastern Oregon, he became intensely interested in the area and began to buy Oregon land. A series of drought years and terrible winters between 1887 and 1890 resulted in many bankruptcies. Meanwhile some of John Devine's land acquisitions were declared illegal, forcing him to repurchase the properties. In 1888-89 he lost more than three-fourths of his stock and declared bankruptcy. Miller was the sole bidder for the Devine estate. He acquired the property, which included about 150,000 acres of land, and retained Devine as manager.

But when the two cattle barons failed to get along, Miller, who was always careful with his money—to the point of being miserly, gave Devine a life-time, nontransferable ownership of the 6,000-acre Alvord Ranch—fully stocked with livestock. This puzzling act of generosity was totally out of keeping with Miller's nature. After Devine's death, Miller and Lux leased the Alvord Ranch, and it was home base for John Gilcrest who managed Miller's operations in Oregon and northern Nevada. Besides the Alvord Ranch, Miller came to own the Juniper Lake, Mann Lake, Serrano, and Whitehorse ranches east of Steens Mountain, plus a series of ranches, including the Island Ranch, extending up the Silvies Valley and along the Malheur River. After taking over Devine's property, Miller organized his holdings into the gigantic Pacific Land and Livestock Company.

Innumerable stories and anecdotes are told about Miller. He was uneducated, lacking in social graces, and had a poor command of the English language. Some historians have labeled him a butcher rather than a cattleman. But Miller had all the essential qualities for success in his chosen endeavor, which seems to have been his sole interest in life. He was shrewd, an uncanny judge of men and business opportunities, and tough in a bargain. He has been described as greedy and stubborn, yet, rather than cultivate enemies, he knowingly let settlers and others steal cattle to start herds and feed hungry families. Miller insisted that all animals be treated well, and every traveler could count on a meal at any of his ranches. Miller's encyclopedic mind and attention to minutia have evoked much derisive humor, such as when he examined kitchen garbage at his various ranches for evidence of wastefulness. But it is significant that after his death and without his financial genius and careful management, the world's largest cattle empire dissolved in a few years.

When the mines opened in Oregon and Idaho, miners demanded and could afford good red meat. A few cattle were brought from western Oregon, but most came from California. In 1867 a herd of about 1,000 longhorns was driven from Texas to southeastern Idaho. Other herds of longhorns were brought from Texas in 1868, and a gigantic herd of 10,000 came up in 1869. Because there were no fences, cattle, which were not winter fed, rapidly populated open ranges. By the early 1880's Oregon cattle numbered at least 800,000 head, and many ranges around Steens Mountain and elsewhere in eastern Oregon were overstocked. Some of the excess cattle were sold and driven to other states. In 1879, Clarence King set out for Medicine Bow, Wyoming, with 12,000 steers from the Steens area, some belonging to French and Miller. Because of Indian intervention and a harsh winter, about 7,000 steers were lost along the way. Other cattle drives terminated at points as far away as Kansas and Missouri.

Sheep arrived about the same time as cattle, and by the 1890's were more numerous than cattle. Unlike cattlemen, most sheepherders and owners, many of whom were Irish or Basque, owned no land, but took flocks to the mountains in summer and returned to desert lowlands in winter. Although the open range was free for the taking, animosity flared between cattlemen and sheepmen, and "Sheep Shooter" organizations formed in some areas. The Crook County Sheep Shooters brazenly reported their annual "tallys" to Portland newspapers. In 1901 conservative estimates placed over 140,000 sheep on Steens Mountain—by 1971 the number was reduced to 6,000, and in 1972 sheep were banned, although cattle continued to graze the mountain.

While many sought and found fortune in cattle and sheep, William Walter (Bill) Brown, who operated in the vast expanse of desert between Bend and Burns, became "Horse King" of the West. Brown owned 38,000 acres, 22,000 sheep, and 10,000 horses, and grazed his stock 150 miles in every direction from the ranch headquarters.

Every cowhand needed a string of four to ten horses, and the growing West used horses for every task. Oregon horses were prized and sold all over the United States. In 1917 in a single sale, Brown delivered 1,000 horses to the U.S. Cavalry, receiving $100 each for geldings and $85 for mares. The French and British armed forces also bought horses from Brown, who was reported to have made a million dollars several times. But Brown's eccentricity and generosity prevented him from keeping wealth. He gave large sums to charities and was noted for checks written on anything at hand—a scrap of newspaper, a label from a tin can, etc. A store on his home ranch was left unattended, and customers were supposed to leave payment in a cigar box! Oregon's horse population peaked at about 400,000 during World War I, not counting the thousands that ran wild. Bill Brown came to the desert in 1882 and died at 86 in 1941.

A railroad from California reached Winnemucca in 1867 and continued on to Promontory Point, Utah where it met the line coming from the East in 1869. Gold and silver spikes were driven to commemorate completion of the first transcontinental railway. Another transcontinental line reached Ontario in 1883 and Huntington in 1885. A branch line came to Crane in 1916 and was extended to Burns in 1924.

The first Homestead Act, entitling a citizen to 160 acres, was signed by President Lincoln in 1862. The Act required at least 7 months residence on the claim each year for 5 years, construction of a habitable house, and cultivation of at least 20 acres of the 160. By paying $1.25 per acre, one could acquire ownership in only 14 months. By 1878 most of the choice land was taken, leaving only the dry desert. In 1909 a new Homestead Act entitled homesteaders to 320 acres of non-irrigable land, later increased to 640 in 1916 legislation. Responding to the government's generosity, thousands of homesteaders began flocking to the desert in about 1909. Civic organizations, chambers of commerce, and railroads launched promotional campaigns to entice homesteaders.

In Catlow Valley small settlements named Beckley, Blitzen, Berdugo, Ragtown, and Sageview sprang up. The population of the valley grew to 700, including 200 voters. By 1921 most of the would be dry-land farmers had starved out and left, selling land for as little as 10¢ per acre.

South of Wright's Point, settlement of Sunset Valley began in

1906. By 1914 the community had 57 registered voters—all male—and could boast the largest rural school in Harney County. After 1915 the population dwindled, and today, only a tiny cemetery hidden in greasewood thickets marks the spot. A list of 25 ghost towns in southeastern Oregon reveals that all were granted post offices between 1906 and 1917, and that all of them closed after an average existence of less than 8 years. The Homestead Acts were finally repealed in 1976.

Most homesteaders suffered severely. Many survived on a diet of jackrabbits, which were plentiful. In 1915, when Harney County offered a bounty of 5¢ each for jackrabbits, shocked officials paid $51,459.10 for 1,029,182 rabbits. Between 1862 and 1934, an area larger than Delaware was open to homesteaders in Harney County, but the land was unclaimed and remains a part of the public domain.

Besides the Homestead Act, other legislation permitted citizens to obtain title to public lands for forestry, mining, livestock, and irrigation. An Oregon act of 1870 made overflow and swampland available for a pittance, and much excellent land was obtained fraudulently under this act. Tales are told of "swampland" claims filed after the claimants inspected the land in a boat—aboard a wagon! Devine, French, Miller, and others expanded holdings using every devious scheme. When settlers arrived and found the good land taken, disputes, lawsuits, harassment campaigns, feuds and gun play resulted.

After Indians defeated Custer in 1876 and Chief Joseph embarrassed the United States Army in 1877, the Bannocks, led by Buffalo Horn, went on the warpath in 1878. Their major grievance was loss of a tribal camas harvesting site through error of the clerk who typed the treaty. Many Northern Paiutes, under Chief Egan, joined the Bannocks, destroyed property in the Harney Basin, and fought a pitched battle with troops and local citizens on Silver Creek, where Egan was badly wounded. Before the uprising, Malheur Paiutes had been placed on a reservation of 2,285 square miles. Ostensibly because the Indians would not return to the reservation, but actually because white men coveted the lands, all but one square mile was returned to the public domain in 1883. Henry Miller obtained a sizeable chunk of the land.

In 1856 all of eastern Oregon was in one gigantic county, Wasco, which included 130,000 square miles extending from the Cascades to the Rockies. Grant County was founded in 1864 and divided into Grant and Harney counties in 1889. Lake County was formed in 1874 and included Klamath County. Baker County was divided to form Baker and Malheur counties in 1887. Burns, named after the famous Scottish poet, acquired a post office in 1884 and was incorporated in 1889. Harney was the first county seat of Harney County, but lost the distinction to Burns in 1890, after the Oregon Supreme Court ruled that Burns had won a contested election by a six-vote margin.

The first white child born in the area that is now Harney County was Jennie Lucas, born 10 April 1868, at Fort Harney. John Smyth, who crossed the Harney Basin with a wagon train in 1853, returned and settled at Warm Springs, the site currently occupied by the Edward Hines Lumber Mill. There a daughter, Margaret, was born in 1873—the first child born to a non-military resident. Later the Smyth family moved to Happy Valley (near Diamond), where John and his father George lost their lives when Indians surrounded and burned their house during the Bannock uprising.

In 1864-67 the Oregon Central Military Road was established to shorten the distance from Lane County, Oregon to Fort Boise. Land grants were made to complete the Willamette Valley and Cascade Mountain Wagon Road from Albany to Idaho in 1864-67. Its 448-mile route passed Camp Currey and Fort Harney, and the company was later hauled into court for having done a minimal job. The Central Oregon Wagon Route, also established with land grants, extended from the Klamath country to camps Alvord and C.F. Smith and on to Idaho. Horse drawn freight and stage lines coursed along these primitive routes for many years.

The first automobile came to Burns in 1907, signaling the end of an era. In 1929, location and grading was begun for U.S. 20 between Bend and Burns. A road had been built between Burns and Crane in 1920. In 1930 the Canyon City-Burns road was built, and in 1932, U.S. 395 was approved. U.S. 78 to Winnemucca was not completed until the 1950's.

Today Oregon's Great Basin country continues to be dominated by the cattle industry started by the cattle barons. Most of the vast area is publicly owned and managed by various federal agencies. When one stands in a great expanse of empty desert, it is tempting to imagine that the land has never before been trod by man. But given the long and exciting history of the area, a prudent person will likely imagine otherwise.

CHAPTER 5

Plants

The boundaries of the northwestern section of the Great Basin correspond approximately with those of a distinctive vegetational region—the Lake Section. Although a large number of plant species are found in the region, a few sagebrushes, rabbitbrushes, chenopods, and native bunchgrasses dominate the vegetation, which is sometimes called Northern Desert Scrub. The flora derives its distinctiveness and character from the environmental restrictions imposed by dryness, thin volcanic soils, and extensive accumulations of alkali. Within the confines of these general environmental limits, the distribution of local plant communities reflects soil depth and fertility, soil moisture and drainage, slope, exposure, elevation, acidity, salinity, temperature extremes, and other ecological factors.

Floral elements from the Rocky Mountains, Cascade-Sierra ranges, Great Basin, and more northerly regions meet on some higher mountains, such as Steens Mountain, and form a complicated mixture of plants. The life zone scheme, which has some theoretical imperfections, is nevertheless a useful way of designating altitudinal zones of vegetation in the region. Because coniferous forests are poorly developed or absent on the mountain ranges and because life zones are sharply distorted by being higher on warmer, southern slopes and lower on northern slopes, the life zones are sometimes difficult to recognize.

The Upper Sonoran Zone, extending from about 4,000 to 5,000 feet, is distinguished by desert scrub species such as sagebrushes (particularly tall sage), greasewood, saltbushes, rabbitbrushes, and in higher places, Western juniper. From about 5,000 to 7,000 feet, the Transition Zone, basically treeless except for high-ranging juniper and low-ranging mountain mahogany, consists of open slopes, with tall sage on better soils and low sage on poorer sites. The Canadian Zone (7,000 to 8,000 feet) is easily recognized by its mountain mahogany on drier exposed ridges, aspen in protected ravines, and open expanses of mixed low sage and bunchgrasses. The Hudsonian Zone (8,000 to 9,000 feet) is primarily a region populated with subalpine bunchgrasses and forbs, including many summer wildflowers. The Arctic-Alpine Zone, if actually present, is restricted to small areas above 9,000 feet.

The best way to deal with the region's plants is to consider natural assemblages of species that constitute distinct plant communities. Between the bottoms of interior basins and the crests of adjacent mountain ranges are numerous plant communities characterized by distinct appearance, relatively constant species composition, and predictable spatial relationships to one another. The system of plant communities used in the following discussions was selected for convenience and simplicity—it is not a formally recognized classification and may not suit the fancy of more knowledgeable plant ecologists.

Malheur Lake (elevation about 4,100 feet) is actually a freshwater marsh whose greatest depth seldom exceeds six feet, even when the lake reaches its maximal size of about 67,000 acres. The chemical composition of the water ranges from moderately alkaline (pH 7.9) in the western portion to highly alkaline (pH 8.6) along the eastern margin. Scattered throughout the marsh are areas of open water supporting masses of submergent plants such as sago pondweed (*Potamogeton pectinatus*), horned pondweed (*Zannichellia palustris*), water milfoil (*Myriophyllum spicatum*), and various others. Sago pondweed is an important and tremendously productive waterfowl food, and the submergent plants attract large aggregations of coots, ducks, geese, and swans during good years. Use is particularly intense during the spring and fall migrations. Whenever the level of the lakes recedes sufficiently to permit aeration of bottom sediments, increased production of submerged plants follows—thus making the lake more attractive to waterfowl in ensuing years.

Elsewhere in the lake, where water is more shallow, emergent plants protrude above the water and create immense acreages of virtually impenetrable vegetation. Some major species of emergents are hardstem bulrush (*Scirpus acutus*), cattail (*Typha latifolia*), burreed (*Sparganium eurycarpum*), and Baltic rush (*Juncus balticus*). Emergent vegetation provides important muskrat habitat and supports nesting colonies of herons, cormorants, egrets, and other birds. In some years, muskrat populations in Malheur Lake have exceeded 50,000, and as many as 20,000 per year have been trapped.

Near ponds and lakes and elsewhere in lower portions of interior basins where soils are relatively free of alkali, lowland meadows occur. These meadows, when naturally flooded by spring runoff or intentionally irrigated, hold standing water for brief periods in late spring and early summer. These are the wild hay meadows which

33

provide the principal source of cattle feed in winter. Many mammals and birds use the meadow habitat for cover, nesting, and feeding. Sedges (several species of *Carex*), rushes (e.g. *Eleocharis palustris*), a few grasses such as meadow barley (*Hordeum brachyantherum*), and other plants, like water plantain and broadleaved arrowhead, dominate moist meadows.

Riparian or stream-side vegetation, particularly trees and shrubs, tends to be sparse on the floors of desert basins, and if present, is usually limited to patches of willows (*Salix sp.*) and an occasional black cottonwood (*Populus trichocarpa*). Near the mouths of canyons, where streams spill out into basins, a more diversified zone of alder (*Alnus sp.*) dogwood (*Cornus sp.*), currant (*Ribes sp.*), chokecherry (*Prunus sp.*), and elderberry (*Sambucus sp.*) may border streams. Great horned owls, magpies, and many songbirds nest in riparian habitat. Beavers depend largely upon willow and cottonwood for winter food sources, and mule deer browse and use willow thickets for cover during the fall and early winter.

Some of the most distinctive plant communities in arid regions are associated with high alkalinity. Alkali, consisting of calcium carbonate, sodium salts, and various other compounds, leaches from volcanic rocks and washes into playas and other poorly drained flatlands, where it remains after the water evaporates. Because of standing water, present during the early spring, and high concentrations of alkali, playas are lifeless salt beds upon which plants are unable to germinate or survive. Harney Lake and the Alvord Desert are good examples.

Although plants cannot grow on playas, some species crowd right to the edge. Desert saltgrass (*Distichlis stricta*) is such a plant and is able to prosper along playa margins—even where a salty crust conceals the soil. Greasewood (*Sarcobatus vermiculatus*) differs from most drab-colored desert shrubs in being bright green and is one of the best indicators of alkaline conditions and requires sites where the roots can penetrate to sources of ground water. Saltbush (*Atriplex confertifolia*) and spiny hopsage (*Grayia spinosa*) are locally abundant in the greasewood community. On slightly higher and less alkaline areas, giant wild rye (*Elymus cinereus*) and rabbitbrush (*Chrysothamnus nauseosus*) are associated with greasewood. In heavily grazed sites, although areas of bare soil are interspersed between greasewood plants, cheatgrass (*Bromus tectorum*), squirreltail barley (*Hordeum jubatum*), and a few other plants find refuge around the bases of the spiny greasewoods. Also, Russian thistle or tumbleweed (*Salsola kali*) may proliferate on disturbed alkaline soils, frequently forming a solid ground cover.

Few animals seek out highly alkaline areas, but black-tailed jackrabbits are sometimes abundant, especially if the greasewood stand is interrupted by hummocks of higher ground supporting tall sage. In some areas these hummocks produce dense stands of giant wild rye, and when near water, they provide favorite nesting sites for mallards.

In hotter, drier valleys a shadscale and saltbush (*Atriplex sp.*) community of salt-tolerant plants occurs with greasewood on alkaline soils and desert pavement. Associated species in this community include winterfat (*Eurotia lanata*), spiny hopsage, and several horsebrushes (*Tetradymia spp.*). Although this assemblage of plants is better represented in the Alvord Basin than in the Harney Basin, the community reaches its best development farther south in Nevada. Antelope ground squirrels, leopard lizards, and desert horned lizards reside in the community.

Slightly above the alkaline communities on better drained and more sandy soils is *Artemisia tridentata*—the famous tall sage. This plant is the Nevada state flower and probably the most widely distributed and abundant plant in the western United States. It grows in a wide range of habitats including the tops of hummocks in alkaline flats, along fringing foothills of basins, over most of the high desert upland and plains, and even well up onto mountain ranges where deeper soils occur. On ideal sites having deep soils and ample water, tall sage may reach a height of 8 feet and assume the appearance of a tree; on dry, rocky, and thin soils it may barely attain a foot in height. In some areas tall sage constitutes 80% of the vegetative stand, and the number of individual plants approaches incredible densities of 6,000 to 7,000 per acre. Although sage has a high protein content, domestic livestock prefer almost any other plant, and therefore, nearly 100 years of grazing and recent success in controlling range fires have strongly favored the dominance of sage. Rabbitbrush, giant wild rye, spiny hopsage, cheatgrass, and bottlebrush squirreltail (*Sitanion hystrix*) are common associates. In less heavily grazed areas, bluebunch wheatgrass (*Agropyron spicatum*), Idaho fescue (*Festuca idahoensis*), and Sandberg's bluegrass (*Poa sandbergii*) are subdominants.

At higher elevations, tall sage is replaced by the short sages, *Artemisia rigida* and *A. arbuscula*. On high desert uplands, wherever small basins of internal drainage are found, a solid stand of silver sage (*A. cana*) often covers playas. These "cana flats" were esteemed by sheepmen and continue to be important forage for cattle. Short sage extends to the summits of many Great Basin ranges, including Steens Mountains.

Sage is an important and nutritious food for pronghorns, winter deer herds, sage grouse, rabbits, and other mammals. Sage sparrows, sage thrashers, and Brewer's sparrows are common songbirds. Because cattle tend to avoid sage and because it crowds out more desirable range plants, extensive tracts of sagelands are sprayed with herbicides by the Bureau of Land Management and seeded with crested wheatgrass (*Agrophyron cristatum*). Crested-wheatgrass seedings provide up to eight times as much forage for cattle as does rangeland supporting sage and native bunchgrasses. Crested wheatgrass, a native of Asia, is competitive, can tolerate heavy grazing, and is long lived—a single clump may live 30 years. Areas burned by range fires are also seeded with crested wheatgrass.

Where buttes, cinder cones, or other landforms rise above basin floors, soils tend to be rocky. On the south slopes of these elevated features, saltbush, spiny hopsage, horsebrush, and greasewood may be codominants, while tall sage and rabbitbrush often dominate north slopes. Indian ricegrass (*Oryzopsis hymenoides*), cheatgrass, and peppergrass (*Lepidium sp.*) are also found.

Most desert basins contain wind-deposited sand dunes. Active dunes of rippled sand are usually devoid of vegetation. On less active sites, sand dock (*Rumex venosus*), tufted evening primrose (*Oenothera caespitosa*), and Indian ricegrass become established. Sand dunes are deficient in nitrogen, thus nitrogen-fixing members of the pea family are also early pioneers on dunes. Rabbitbrush, greasewood, and tall sage invade older sedentary dunes. Following disturbance, such as fire, grazing, or off-road vehicles, wind may damage stabilized dunes, producing sand blow-outs and exposing grotesque and tangled root systems. Often kangaroo mice and leopard lizards are found on dunes.

Near the upper limits of the tall sage zone is a belt of Western juniper (*Juniperus occidentalis*). Isolated trees are sometimes scattered far from the main belt of junipers, in which trees tend to be loosely dispersed in open woodlands, rather than in a closed forest. The best stands often grow on steep slopes, rocky outcrops, and northern exposures. Unlike most trees, the juniper has no identifying shape—every tree being a non-conformist within a broad range of possible variation. Bitterbrush (*Purshia tridentata*), squaw currant (*Ribes cereum*), Oregon grape (*Berberis repens*), and snowberry (*Symphoricarpos oreophilus*) are common associates. Mountain mahogany (*Cercocarpus ledifolius*) appears near the top of the juniper belt, and Idaho fescue finds refuge beneath juniper crowns. The juniper belt is an important wintering area for deer herds.

The riparian vegetation of mountain canyons includes willows, alder, dogwood, black cottonwood, water birch (*Betula fontinalis*), currant, and aspen. At higher elevations, all woody species except willow disappear from stream borders and are replaced by sedges, rushes, monkey flowers (*Mimulus sp.*), and various forbs. Beavers, meadow mice, dippers, and other animals inhabit the edges of mountain streams. Riparian vegetation, by shading streams, preventing erosion, and harboring insects, is essential to the trout fishery.

Near the upper edge of the juniper belt on Steens Mountain, two tributaries of Muddy Creek, Little Fir and Big Fir canyons, support groves of Sierran white fir (*Abies concolor*). Each grove covers about 50 acres and occupies a north slope at elevations between 5,900 and 6,200 feet. The trees are successfully reproducing, and the stands form a closed canopy that effectively excludes other plants from the forest floor. The oldest trees are about 300 years old. The absence of other conifers on Steens Mountain is puzzling, but may be attributed to past fires and glaciation. A few Sierran white firs are also found on Hart Mountain and the East Warner Mountains. Small isolated acreages of ponderosa pine (*Pinus ponderosa*) occur on Bald Mountain near the East Warner Mountains and in five canyons on the west side of Hart Mountain. Although the Hart Mountain pines are reproducing, nearly all the larger trees are severely diseased. White bark pine (*Pinus albicaulis*) grows on the Pine Forest Range, and a subalpine forest of limber pine (*P. flexilis*) is present on the Santa Rosa Range. Between Burns and the summit of the Strawberry Mountains, all the classical zones of coniferous forest can be seen (see Tour #10, Chapter 11).

In and above the juniper belt are numerous rock outcrops, talus slopes, and cliffs. Although these areas support a diverse vegetation, serviceberry (*Amelanchier sp.*), bitter cherry (*Prunus emarginata*), squaw currant, dwarf juniper (*Juniperus communis*), mountain mahogany, penstemons (*Penstemon sp.*), and buckwheats (*Eriogonum sp.*) are most common. Many of the exposed rock surfaces are covered with patches of crustose lichens. In places lichens are sufficiently abundant to color entire canyon walls with brilliant hues of chartreuse, yellow, orange, red, and rust. Animals in these rocky habitats include marmots, golden-mantled ground squirrels, woodrats, pikas, and rock wrens. Woodrats use the same urinating stations repeatedly, thus creating large white deposits of urine residues on the rimrocks. These deposits, often readily visible from roads and highways, are a rich source of nitrogen and appear to stimulate growth and colonization of crustose lichens, thus enhancing the color of desert rims.

Perhaps the most beautiful and scenic sights on mountain ranges of the northern Great Basin are the pristine groves of quaking aspen (*Populus tremuloides*). Aspen leaves are borne on laterally flattened petioles that permit the leaves to "quake" or tremble in even the slightest breeze. The handsome white trunks and rustling sound of tremoring leaves generate a serenity that is not soon forgotten. Unfortunately, the smooth white bark has tempted generations of the uncouth to carve initials and other defacing trivia. Aspens, which may grow to 65 feet, send out roots that sprout and give rise to new trees, thus a clone of trees develops from one "parent." When fungus successfully attacks one tree, it may quickly spread to others and cause the entire grove to die almost simultaneously. In autumn, aspens put on an incredible display of fall colors ranging from dazzling yellows to brilliant reds. Small sage, snowberry, and numerous herbs are commonly part of the aspen community. Mountain bluebirds, Cassin's finches, several woodpeckers, other songbirds, yellow pine chipmunks, and many small rodents make their homes in aspen groves.

At intermediate elevations, numerous mountain meadows have formed, many originating as shallow glacial lakes which are gradually filling with accumulated sediments and organic matter. This results in concentric zones of plants encroaching upon the lake, a process called hydrarch succession, classically illustrated at Lily Lake on Steens Mountain. In the final stages of the process, a bog forms in which fringing willows and zones of sedges, rushes, aquatic buttercups (*Ranunculus sp.*), and other plants are evident (e.g., Whorehouse Meadows on Steens Mountain).

In drier meadows, false hellebore (*Veratrum californicum*), false Solomon's seal (*Smilacina racemosa*), and a fantastic assemblage of other flowering plants make a showy summer scene. Belding's ground squirrels, meadow mice, and shrews are common mammals inhabiting mountain meadows.

Above the zone of aspen are wide-open spaces of subalpine grasslands. Soils are shallow and often bare in much of this zone. Short sage is abundant in the lower reaches, but becomes uncommon at higher elevations. Numerous grasses, lupines (*Lupinus sp.*), buckwheats, locoweeds (*Astragalus sp.*), paintbrushes (*Castilleja sp.*), and an array of other herbaceous species are present. Many of the plants are dwarfed and prostrate, and do not bloom until mid or late summer. Conspicuous animals include Belding's ground squirrels and horned larks. Glacial cirques in this zone may contain steer's head bleeding hearts (*Dicentra uniflora*), alpine shooting stars (*Dodecatheon alpinum*), buttercups, and sedges. The flower-filled cirques are Nature's formal gardens.

The summit of Steens Mountain is characterized by rocky areas, shallow soil, and minimal vegetative cover. Low locoweeds, yarrow (*Achillea millefolium*), shrubby cinquefoil (*Potentilla fruticosa*), Oregon silene (*Silene oregana*), onion (*Allium sp.*), and others are present. Several species of ferns occur along rims forming the head wall of Wildhorse Gorge, and lichens adorn most exposed rims. White-throated swifts, rosy finches, and golden-mantled ground squirrels spend brief summers at these elevations.

The numerous thermal hot springs of the desert represent a special environment in which heat-tolerant blue-green algae flourish. Certain species tolerate extremely high temperatures (tolerated temperatures range up to 185°F), but are replaced by less tolerant species as water cools downstream. Because of the spectrum of colors exhibited by various algae, the color photographer can have a field day near thermal pools. An opposite extreme involves green algae which live in and impart a red tint to the permanent snowfields on mountains of the Great Basin.

Many of the typical plants of alkaline areas fail to range north of the Harney Basin, or occur sparingly in a few isolated areas such as the Powder Valley. Others such as Mormon tea (*Ephedra viridis*), iodine bush (*Allenrolfea occidentalis*), and one of the four-o-clocks (*Mirabilis bigelovii* var. *retrorsa*) are found in the Alvord Basin, but no farther north. Mormon tea contains an alkaloid drug, ephedrine, which is an antidepressant and anticongestant. The plant was used as a tea and remedy by settlers and Paiutes. The following plants are some of the endemics found In Oregon's Great Basin country: *Agastache cusickii var. cusickii, Castilleja steenensis, Cirsium peckii, Draba sphaeroides var. cusickii, Eriogonum cusickii, Eriogonum umbellatum var. glaberrimum, and Penstemon davidsonii var. praeteritus.* Because several of these plants are rare or endangered, they should not be collected or disturbed.

Harsh environmental conditions severely limit the selection of trees that can be planted as ornamental or shade trees around ranches and other settlements in the high desert. In moist, deep soils that are relatively free of alkali, poplars are favored for shade and as effective windbreaks. Others include cottonwoods, boxelders, willows, Siberian elms, and spruces. On drier more difficult sites, Russian olive, juniper, black locust, and hackberry may grow. But there are some places where planting a tree is a senseless and futile act!

The evolutionary development of the flora of the northern Great Basin is an epic story of fantastic changes. After the ancient seas receded, tropical vegetation invaded and was eventually replaced by a subtopical flora when a cooling trend developed. By early Miocene times (20 to 25 million years ago), interior basins became drier and cooler, the subtropical flora retreated southward, and sagebrush arrived in the area—as shown by fossil pollen. In late Miocene times a mixed forest of conifers and deciduous hardwoods prevailed, while a semiarid vegetation of live oaks and chaparral occupied drier sites. By the early Pliocene (10 to 13 million years ago), savanna and grasslands were extensive, with maples, cottonwoods, and other species bordering streams, and chaparral dominating drier sites. The shift toward a desert flora had taken place by late Pliocene times, but the change was not to be completed until after the pulvial lakes disappeared at the end of the Pleistocene. Miocene and Pliocene beds of plant fossils are found in the Trout Creek Mountains, along the base of the Steens Mountain scarp, and at several other locations.

Visitors to the Great Basin, especially those from areas of heavy rainfall west of the Cascade-Sierra Range, are dismayed or even depressed by the absence of trees. The superficial tourist who fills his gas tank and hurriedly drives on in search of trees cannot be blamed. But those who stay a few days in the desert eventually stop searching for trees and begin to see what *is* present—a wonderfully diverse and fantastically interesting assemblage of desert-adapted plants—tough but fragile—nondescript from a distance but intricate up close. These discerning people are likely to be "hooked" and will probably return again and again.

CHAPTER 6

Animals

The northern Great Basin is the home of an immensely diverse assemblage of animals. The richness of the fauna reflects the region's diversity of available habitats. Differences in terrain, vegetation, moisture, elevation, soils, and many other ecological factors produce complex patterns of animal distribution. Weather, seasonal changes, and stage of life history may further modify distributional patterns. While some species restrict their activities to a single, well-defined plant community, others may ignore community boundaries and use resources found in two or more plant communities. Indeed, some animals range freely, showing little preference for a specific habitat.

Because excellent and inexpensive field guides and taxonomic references are available, the identification and regional distribution of animals will not be emphasized here. Instead, the reader is advised of the animals to be expected in the area and provided information about the ecology and habits of typical representatives of the desert fauna—especially the larger, more conspicuous species.

Mammals:

Although more than 85 species of mammals are found in Oregon's Great Basin country, many are confined to forested portions of upland drainages and are not really a part of the high desert environment. For example, many mammals typical of the Blue Mountains occur in the upper reaches of the Silvies River—technically within the Great Basin. These peripheral species are included, but assigned a minor role in the discussion.

The Order Insectivora (shrews and moles) is poorly represented in arid regions. Four species of shrews (Family Soricidae) are found in the northern Great Basin, including Preble's shrew (*Sorex preblei*), the vagrant shrew (*Sorex vagrans*), the water shrew (*Sorex palustris*), and Merriam's shrew (*Sorex merriami*). Preble's and vagrant shrews inhabit well-watered locations having an abundance of concealing cover. Water shrews live along swift streams and other water at higher elevations. Merriam's shrew is found in undisturbed sagebrush-bunchgrass habitats.

Shrews, the smallest of the mammals, are notable for their enormous appetites, hyperactivity, and secretive ways. They feed primarily on invertebrates, mice, and lizards, but even larger animals are quite acceptable. Shrews, especially females with young, may consume their own weight in food every few hours and will quickly die of exposure if deprived of an energy source. The young, usually five or six and no larger than honeybees at birth, are weaned when scarcely a month old. Although shrews are sometimes caught in traps, they are seldom seen.

Moles (Family Talpidae) are conspicuously absent in the high desert. These accomplished burrowers spend most of their lives underground feeding on grubs, earthworms, and other invertebrates. The broad-footed mole (*Scapanus latimanus*) invades open, semi-arid areas along the western edge of the Great Basin in south-central Oregon.

Bats (Order Chiroptera) include a large and diverse group of tropical species plus many less spectacular forms in temperate regions. Flight, echo-location, and a rich folklore make bats among the most fascinating of all creatures. In the northern Great Basin there are 13 species of evening bats (Family Vespertilionidae): little brown bat (*Myotis lucifugus*), Yuma brown bat (*Myotis yumanensis*), long-eared brown bat (*Myotis evotis*), long-legged brown bat (*Myotis volans*), California brown bat (*Myotis californicus*), small-footed brown bat (*Myotis subulatus*), silver-haired bat (*Lasionycteris noctivagans*), Western pipistrel (*Pipistrellus hesperus*), big brown bat (*Eptesicus fuscus*), hoary bat (*Lasiurus cinereus*), spotted bat (*Euderma maculatum*), Townsend's big-eared bat (*Plecotus townsendi*), and pallid bat (*Antrozous pallidus*).

Most desert bats live at relatively low elevations in cliffs, crevices, caves, or around human dwellings. Because of insect abundance and a continuing need to replenish lost body fluids, bats often occur near water. Bats feed in flight, usually during twilight or darkness. Some species become torpid in winter and move to hibernating sites—others migrate southward. Copulation occurs during fall or winter, sperm are stored until fertilization takes place in the spring, and usually a single young (but up to four) is born in early summer. Initially the young cling to the female and accompany her on foraging trips, but older young remain behind. Bats are important economically in insect control and should not be handled carelessly because of the possibility of rabies.

Rabbits and their relatives (Order Lagomorpha) are well represented in the northern Great Basin. The pika (*Ochotona princeps*) is the only member of its family (Ochotonidae) in the area. Pikas, which resemble small, short-eared rabbits, live in talus slopes and lava beds, usually at higher elevations. They are best known for curing haystacks of vegetation for winter use, a squeaking alarm call that has ventriloquist qualities, and an uncanny ability to "hide" by remaining motionless in plain view.

Rabbits and hares (Family Leporidae) are represented by five species: the pygmy rabbit (*Brachylagus idahoensis*), a small rabbit inhabiting dense stands of tall sage; Nuttall's cottontail (*Sylvilagus nuttalli*); snowshoe hare (*Lepus americanus*), found in forested areas of the southern Blue Mountains; white-tailed jackrabbit (*Lepus townsendi*), which frequents open bunchgrass lands at intermediate elevations; and black-tailed jackrabbit (*Lepus californicus*).

If one were to choose the most typical mammal of the northern Great Basin, the honor might well go to the black-tailed jackrabbit. Staggering along a well-worn rabbit trail with enormous scoop-like ears measuring fully one-third the body length, a jackrabbit (actually a hare) may seem an apt subject for derisive remarks. But when danger threatens, the jack transforms instantly into a fantastic running machine—bounding more than four yards per jump with every 4th or 5th being a high leap that enables the jackrabbit to observe the progress of its pursuer.

Jackrabbits consume almost all types of vegetation, especially grasses, and are active from before sunset to sunrise. They do not burrow, but spend the day resting in a shallow form scratched out beneath a shrub, or even in a clearing. The young, usually two or three per litter, arrive fully haired, with open eyes, and relatively short ears. Populations fluctuate in cycles averaging 7 years (5 to 10 years). In 1915 Harney County, Oregon paid 5 cents bounty each for 1,029,182 scalps, and the jackrabbit population for all of eastern Oregon was once estimated at 20 million. Coyotes, disease, parasites, and adverse weather are natural controlling mechanisms. Although jackrabbits are considered pests on ranges and croplands, they are valuable as buffer species in reducing predation on other types of wildlife. Jackrabbits were a necessity to the Paiutes, who used the fur for warm winter clothing.

The majority of the mammals found in the northern Great Basin are rodents (Order Rodentia), represented by 39 species in 9 families. Rodents are primarily small herbivores and constitute the basic food supply of mammalian predators, birds of prey, and many snakes.

The squirrels and their relatives (Family Sciuridae) are major faunal elements, with one or more species occuring in most areas. Species present are the least chipmunk (*Eutamius minimus*), yellow pine chipmunk (*Eutamius amoenus*), yellow-bellied marmot (*Marmota flaviventris*), white-tailed antelope ground squirrel (*Ammospermophilus leucurus*), Townsend's ground squirrel (*Spermophilus townsendi*), Richardson's ground squirrel (*Spermophilus richardsoni*), Belding's ground squirrel (*Spermophilus beldingi*), Columbian ground squirrel (*Spermophilus columbianus*), golden-mantled ground squirrel (*Spermophilus lateralis*), red squirrel (*Tamiasciurus hudsonicus*), Douglas' squirrel (*Tamiasciurus douglasi*), and Northern flying squirrel (*Glaucomys sabrinus*). The Columbian ground squirrel, red squirrel, Douglas' squirrel, and Northern flying squirrel are all peripheral species restricted to forested mountainous areas.

On unbearably hot days, visitors to the Alvord Basin may glimpse a ghostly flash of white scampering through desert shrubs and rising waves of heat. The white is likely to be the exposed *undersurface* of the tail of an antelope ground squirrel, which uniquely carries the tail arched over its back. This species seems to prefer the hottest, driest, and most hostile desert environments in the Great Basin—even Death Valley. Although antelope ground squirrels stay in their burrows to avoid bad weather, few if any hibernate, as do most ground squirrels, and some remain active even when several inches of snow cover the ground. Drinking is not essential, although water is taken when available, and a diet of insects may supplement a scant water supply during the dry season. Seeds are the principal food and are stored, but invertebrates and flesh are also relished. Great distances are traveled in food gathering.

Usually the females bear a single litter of 6 to 10 young each year. Burrows are generally oval at the entrance, unmarked because the excavated material is scattered, and located in rocky soil that thwarts digging predators. Antelope ground squirrels often climb shrubs to sunbathe or inspect their surroundings. Because of their habitat preferences, these squirrels are of minimal economic importance; certain other ground squirrels are often considered agricultural pests.

Pocket gophers (Family Geomyidae) are represented by Townsend's pocket gopher (*Thomomys townsendi*) and the Northern pocket gopher (*Thomomys talpoides*). These amazing excavators, named for their fur-lined cheek pouches, are active all year. They feed principally on the underground portions of plants. In sandy soil a gopher can tunnel more than 200 feet in a night and amass incredible mounds of soil around a burrow entrance.

Perhaps the most appealing and fascinating desert rodents are the pocket mice and kangaroo rats (Family Heteromyidae). Species present are the little pocket mouse (*Perognathus longimembris*),

Great Basin pocket mouse (*Perognathus parvus*), dark kangaroo mouse (*Microdipodops megacephalus*), Ord's kangaroo rat (*Dipodomys ordi*), chisel-toothed kangaroo rat (*Dipodomys microps*), and Heerman's kangaroo rat (*Dipodomys heermanni*)—the latter species reaching only the western fringe of the Great Basin in the Klamath area.

Pocket mice are remarkably well adapted to desert living. They are small—in fact the little pocket mouse is the smallest North American rodent—nocturnal, and quick. Their burrows often extend 6 or 7 feet below the surface and usually branch into a maze of side tunnels and food storage chambers. Pocket mice, while standing erect, deftly stuff their external cheek pouches with seeds—their favorite food—then rush to cache them and return for another load. The front feet are used to fill and empty the pouches, the latter operation being accomplished by pressure applied to the rear of the bulging pouch. When faced with danger, the pocket mouse will hastily empty its pouches to gain speed for the escape.

Many kinds of seeds are gathered before desert winds can scatter them. Insects are also eaten. Pocket mice have lived 7 years in captivity without drinking. These animals, however, will drink when water is available. Overgrazing, by favoring seed producing weeds at the expense of grasses, may increase pocket mouse populations. Not only must the pocket mouse avoid the usual long list of predators, but it must also beware of its assassin cousins, the grasshopper and white-footed mice.

The kangaroo rat, with its enlarged hind legs, weak forelegs, and long bannered tail, is a unique and lovable character of American deserts. Neither rat nor kangaroo, this enigmatic biped accepts human friendship, but may kill its own kind when several are forced together.

Roo rats are nocturnal, even to the extent of shunning a full moon. As with many nocturnal animals, kangaroo rats are most active early in the night and again before daylight. Using their fur-lined cheek pouches, they compulsively gather seeds until the total supply has been stored. More than 100 quarts of seeds were found in one burrow. Greens and insects are also eaten. Although kangaroo rats may drink from dew drops or rain puddles, a source of free water is not required.

Their complicated maze of subterranean tunnels and chambers is often marked by a large mound of excavated soil containing as many as a dozen entrances. A listener at one of these entrances may be scolded by a thumping sound as the occupant stomps its hind feet.

Kangaroo rats have many enemies, but are extremely alert and

45

may escape would-be captors by resorting to a zig-zag stride that is unpredictable in both direction and distance. A litter usually contains two to five young, and populations may flourish in weedy, overgrazed sites.

We kept a pet kangaroo rat and gave it free run of the house. When "Roo' gathered nearly a cupful of dead flies on the sun porch and stashed them beneath a chair, we thought it humorous. But when a large area of shag rug was clipped for nesting material, "Roo" was ushered back to the wild.

The beaver (*Castor fiber*) is the only North American member of the Family Castoridae. Exploitation of the beaver provided much of the economic incentive for opening the West. Today, under legal protection, beavers are again plentiful. Because food trees are often scarce at lower elevations in the Great Basin, beavers are mostly restricted to upstream locations.

Seven species of cricetid mice and rats (Family Cricetidae) are found in the region. They are the Western harvest mouse (*Reithrodontomys megalotis*), canyon mouse (*Peromyscus crinitus*), common deer mouse (*Peromyscus maniculatus*), pinyon mouse (*Peromyscus truei*), Northern grasshopper mouse (*Onychomys leucogaster*), desert woodrat (*Neotoma lepida*), and bushy-tailed woodrat (*Neotoma cinerea*). Although most of these are widely distributed, the pinyon mouse occurs only in the western edge of the Great Basin in Oregon.

The grasshopper mouse appears to be an ordinary small mouse. But when hungry, it becomes a vicious hunter—not unlike a weasel—and will attack, kill, and devour many kinds of small rodents, including other grasshopper mice. Unable to run down swift prey, they often hunt from ambush and leave only a few scraps and bits after feasting on a kill. Beetles, grasshoppers, and other arthropods (including an occasional scorpion) round out the diet.

Woodrats are known for collecting trivia—thus the name "pack rat". Stolen articles include such diverse items as sticks of dynamite, false teeth, jewelry, and nearly every small object known to man. These paraphernalia and great quantities of sticks, bones, and other debris are incorporated into the malodorous nest. Woodrats are nocturnal and feed primarily on vegetable foods. Although woodrats are handsome and well groomed, they suffer from being mistakenly compared with their distant relatives—the Old World rats.

The voles (Family Microtidae) are a large group of unusually chunky, short-tailed mice. Because most species inhabit meadows or marshes, they are poorly represented in arid regions. Species in the northern Great Basin include Gapper's red-backed mouse

(*Clethrionomys gapperi*), the heather mouse (*Phenacomys intermedius*), montane meadow mouse (*Microtus montanus*), long-tailed meadow mouse (*Microtus longicaudus*), Richardson's water vole (*Arvicola richardsoni*), sagebrush vole (*Lagurus curtatus*), and muskrat (*Ondatra zibethicus*).

The red-backed mouse, heather mouse, and water vole are found only in forested areas along the mountainous northern extremities of the Great Basin. Only the sagebrush vole, the lightest colored of all voles, prefers an arid sagebrush habitat. The muskrat, an important fur-bearer, is a major factor in marsh ecology, and their houses often provide nesting platforms for geese and other waterfowl. Voles constitute a main source of food for nearly all types of predators.

The Old World rats and mice (Family Muridae) have been introduced to North America. Today the Norway rat (*Rattus norvegicus*) and house mouse (*Mus musculus*) may occur wherever human settlements are found. These species easily move from place to place as stowaways in commerce.

The Western jumping mouse (*Zapus princeps*) is the only member of its family (Dipodidae) in the Great Basin. As the name implies, this species has a kangaroo-type locomotion. Jumping mice live around moist areas, usually at high elevations.

The porcupine (*Erethizon dorsatum*) belongs to the Family Erethizontidae. Although most often found in open coniferous forests, porcupines occur widely in the Great Basin, even in sagebrush far from trees. Because of damage to trees and other types of human property, porcupines are often considered pests. Although dogs and wild predators may sustain painful injuries from encounters with porcupines, several large predators eat porcupines regularly. The only time we ate mountain lion, a quill turned up in the roast!

The carnivores (Order Carnivora), represented by 19 species in 5 families, arouse more excitement and emotion than any other group of animals. All are predators, and most are large, rare, and extremely wary. To society, the large carnivores are a dilemma—despised, hunted, and feared by many—enjoyed, protected, and admired by others. Because of economics, spurious ethics, and ignorance, man has severely abused many of these magnificent animals. For some, such as the grizzly bear (the last known Oregon specimen was killed in 1931), a shameful extinction is now history.

Great Basin members of the dog family (Canidae) include the coyote (*Canis latrans*), gray wolf (*Canis lupus*), red fox (*Vulpes vulpes*), and kit fox (*Vulpes velox*). Although a gray wolf was killed in Malheur County, Oregon in 1974, this species is probably extinct in the region included in this book. Likewise, the red fox, once found on Steens Mountain and in northern portions of the Harney Basin, is now extremely rare or absent.

The coyote may be the most maligned animal on earth. Thousands of ranchers drive around with high-powered rifles ready, just hoping for a glimpse of this animal, which has been shot, poisoned, trapped, and persecuted by every available means. Yet, it thrives. Thank goodness, for the desert would not be the same without it.

Although coyotes are omnivorous and sample almost any foods available, rabbits and various rodents dominate the diet. Except for family groups, coyotes usually hunt alone and appear to delight in pouncing and sniffing as they go about food gathering. Their conflicts with man are discussed in Chapter 9. Litters of 3 to 19 have been recorded, but 5 or 6 are usual. Reproductive rates and densities tend to reflect jackrabbit abundance.

The kit fox, widely distributed in the arid West, was once abundant in the Northwest, but has been severely victimized by trapping and poisoning programs aimed at coyotes. Today the kit fox barely reaches the hot valleys of southeastern Oregon and is listed as an endangered species in the state. In addition to being rare, these small foxes are shy, swift, nocturnal, and usually holed up in their burrows, and therefore, seldom seen. Kangaroo rats, the staple food, and other rodents and rabbits are captured by stealth and quickness and are often taken to the den to be consumed. There are usually four or five young.

The black bear (*Ursus americanus*) is largely restricted to forested regions along the northern reaches of the Great Basin and is the only living representative of its family (Ursidae) in the region. A skull of a grizzly bear was found in Malheur Lake bed when it was dry in the 1930's, and the species was also once present on Steens Mountain.

The Family Procyonidae is represented by the raccoon (*Procyon lotor*), which occurs widely near streams, lakes, and marshes. Their tracks in mud are often seen, but the secretive raccoon is seldom encountered abroad in daylight.

The mustelids (Family Mustelidae) are an ecologically diverse group of predominantly flesh eaters. Most are valued for their pelts. Of the 10 species found in the basin region, few really prefer arid habitats. Species present are the marten (*Martes americanus*), fisher (*Martes pennanti*), short-tailed weasel (*Mustela erminea*), long-tailed weasel (*Mustela frenata*), mink (*Lutreola lutreola*), wolverine (*Gulo gulo*), badger (*Taxidea taxus*), spotted skunk (*Spilogale putorius*), striped skunk (*Mephitus mephitus*), and the river otter (*Lutra canadensis*). Martens and fishers inhabit forests bordering desert areas and are of no great concern here. The wolverine had been given up as extinct in eastern Oregon, but a single individual miraculously appeared on Steens Mountain in 1975. Although once present in the Harney Basin, river otters have not been seen there during the 20th century.

Badgers seem to be well adapted for life in the desert and enjoy a wide distribution. They seldom venture into daylight. Using their superior digging ability, badgers literally mine hapless rodents. With superb strength, a massive low-slung build, and formidable claws and teeth, the badger is a match for any potential adversary, and most creatures avoid them. Their oval burrow entrances pose hazards to horsemen on the open range. We once saw an adult badger frisk away two inquisitive young by the napes of their necks, when the young refused to leave a situation that parental judgment deemed imprudent.

Cats (Family Felidae) are represented by three species—the mountain lion (*Felis concolor*), lynx (*Lynx lynx*), and the bobcat (*Lynx rufus*). The lynx, formerly a resident of Steens Mountain, is currently restricted to forested areas farther north. Although mountain lions were once more abundant and widely distributed, an occasional sighting still occurs.

The bobcat is the most typical cat of the Oregon desert region. Because of their legal status as a predator (until 1977) and valuable pelts, bobcats have become scarce and in need of protection. Bobcats are shy (unless cornered) and usually seen only after sundown near rocky rims, where they hide by day and hunt rabbits and rodents at night. Porcupines are often eaten. Hunting is primarily visual and may involve extensive nightly forays. Prey is often ambushed or captured by a sudden charge. Usually two or three kittens are born on a cliff or ledge.

The even-toed hooved mammals (Order Artiodactyla) are large, long-legged herbivores—highly esteemed as big game species.

The deer family (Cervidae) is represented by the elk (*Cervus elaphus*) and mule deer (*Odocoileus hemionus*). Elk are usually found in forested habitat, but a small herd has moved into isolated areas on Steens Mountain, probably from the southern Blue Mountains. Mule deer are abundant at high elevations and in well-watered valleys during the summer, but migrate to juniper and sagebrush habitat during the winter. Male elk and deer bear deciduous antlers (i.e., they are shed annually).

The pronghorn (*Antilocapra americanus*) is the only living species in the exclusively North American family Antilocapridae. Pronghorns, also called antelope, are widely distributed in the plains and semiarid areas of the West. They are the swiftest of the American mammals, able to attain speeds up to 70 miles per hour in short bursts. Because of an ability to flash alarm signals by displaying patches of white hairs on the buttocks, pronghorns have been called heliographers. When the rump signals are flashed, a potent musk is released from glands controlled by the same muscles that erect the hairs. Some people can smell the scent from several hundred yards, when winds are favorable.

Unlike members of the deer family, both sexes of pronghorns, have horns, and only the black outer sheath is shed and replaced annually. Despite their horns, pronghorns crawl under wire fences; deer usually jump over them. The fawns (there may be one or two) are agile after a day or so, but usually resort to "freezing" when danger threatens. Pronghorns are principally brush browsers, but feed on tender grasses when available. Although populations were once greatly diminished, they have responded favorably to rigid protection and careful conservation.

The bighorn sheep (*Ovis canadensis*) is the only member of the Family Bovidae (cattle and relatives) in the northern Great Basin. Skulls and other bones of buffalo (*Bison bison*) were recovered from the dry bed of Malheur Lake in the early 1930's.

Bighorn sheep originally lived in suitable rimrock, canyons, and lava beds throughout eastern Oregon. Because of a combination of diseases contacted from domestic sheep, excessive hunting, and natural predation, bighorn sheep were largely exterminated in Oregon by around 1915. The last one killed on Steens Mountain was apparently in 1911. In 1954, 20 bighorns were introduced on Hart Mountain from British Columbia. By 1960 a surplus was available and four (one ram, two ewes, and one ewe lamb) were released on Steens Mountain. In 1961, seven more were released. Today both populations are large enough to support limited hunting. In 1976, 16 of the Hart Mountain sheep were transferred to the Pueblo Mountains.

Bighorns dwell in cliffs and rugged terrain along the high, steep scarps of Hart and Steens mountains. In this setting, their famous sure-footedness and ability to negotiate nearly vertical cliffs are tested daily.

Birds:

About 290 species of birds have been recorded or are likely to occur in Oregon's Great Basin region. The large number of species precludes detailed accounts, except for a few that are of unusual interest. Table 2 is an annotated check list including families, common names of species, status (i.e., resident, migrant, etc.), and general habitat requirements. In using the check list, the reader should bear in mind that: (1) many of the species are accidental wanderers, recorded only once or a few times; (2) certain species are listed as hypothetical and must await confirming field observations (e.g., laughing gull); (3) some of the listed birds are found only in peripheral areas (e.g., along the western fringe of the Great Basin in the mountains of northern California or in sub-alpine forested areas of the Strawberry Mountains at the northern edge of the Great Basin); (4) summer residents at high elevations may be restricted to one habitat, but may be widely distributed and found in entirely different habitats at lower elevations in the winter; (5) although a species may occur throughout the year, summer residents may migrate farther south and be replaced by migrants from northern areas (6) and mild winters and unusual food sources may cause normally migratory species to remain in an area for part or all of the winter.

During spring, Western grebes stage their unique mating antics—posturing, complicated reciprocal acts, and strange rushes across the water's surface (Crump Lake in the Warner Valley and Derrick Lake at Malheur Refuge support breeding colonies). Western grebes are unusually graceful and at home in water, and even nest on floating platforms of vegetation. Once endangered by plume hunters, populations of these remarkable birds have increased under protection.

On land, or even in the water, white pelicans appear awkward, but their grace in soaring flight is unequalled for precision and beauty. Flocks often spend long periods of time in aerial ballets—alternately appearing and disappearing as they present different profiles to earth-bound viewers far below. Pelicans are expert fishermen, sometimes fishing cooperatively by forming a large circle and gradually herding carp or other fish to the center. At the last minute, there is feast and frenzy as the immense bills gather and snap up the bounty. The act of nestlings inserting their bills far down parental gullets to retrieve fish is a sight to behold.

Malheur Refuge is the northern-most nesting locality for the white-faced ibis. With long, decurved bill and unique irridescent plumage, this handsome bird is eagerly sought by "Life Listers" at Malheur Refuge.

The trumpeter swan is the largest bird in North America. Males may weigh as much as 38 pounds, but average only 28 pounds. In 1931 the number of trumpeter swans in the United States was only 35 (others occurred in Canada and Alaska). In the mid-1940's a few swans from a protected population at Red Rock Lake Refuge in Montana were brought to Malheur Refuge, where they soon produced a fairly stable population of 10-20 pairs. Most nest in the Blitzen Valley. Thousands of migrating whistling swans usually make feeding and resting stops on the large lakes of southeastern

Table 2. An annotated check list of birds occurring or expected to occur in the Great Basin region of Oregon and northern Nevada.

Family and Common Name	Status	General Habitat
GAVIIDAE *(Loons)*		
___ Common loon	Migrant	Lakes
___ Arctic loon	Accidental	Lakes
PODICIPEDIDAE *(Grebes)*		
___ Red-necked grebe	Accidental	Lakes
___ Horned grebe	Summer resident	Marshes & ponds
___ Eared grebe	Summer resident	Lakes, marshes & ponds
___ Western grebe	Summer resident	Lakes & marshes
___ Pied-billed grebe	Summer resident	Marshes & ponds
PELECANIDAE *(Pelicans)*		
___ White pelican	Summer resident	Lakes & marshes
PHALACROCORACIDAE *(Cormorants)*		
___ Double-crested cormorant	Summer resident	Lakes
ARDEIDAE *(Herons and Bitterns)*		
___ Great blue heron	Permanent resident	Waterways
___ Cattle egret	Accidental	Pastures
___ Great egret	Summer resident	Marshes & waterways
___ Snowy egret	Summer resident	Marshes & waterways

___ Louisiana heron	Accidental	Waterways & ponds
___ Black-crowned night heron	Summer resident	Marshes & sloughs
___ Least bittern	Rare summer resident	Marshes
___ American bittern	Summer resident	Marshes

THRESKIORNITHIDAE *(Ibises)*

___ White-faced ibis	Summer resident	Meadows & marshes

ANATIDAE *(Swans, Geese, and Ducks)*

___ Whistling swan	Migrant	Lakes
___ Trumpeter swan	Permanent resident	Lakes & ponds
___ Canada goose	Permanent resident	Marshes & fields
___ White-fronted goose	Migrant	Marshes & fields
___ Emperor goose	Accidental	Marshes & fields
___ Snow goose (blue & white phases)	Migrant	Marshes & fields
___ Ross' goose	Migrant	Marshes & fields
___ Mallard	Permanent resident & migrant	Wetlands & waterways
___ Black duck	Accidental	Wetlands & waterways
___ Gadwall	Permanent resident	Waterways & marshes
___ Pintail	Permanent resident	Marshes, fields & ponds
___ Green-winged teal	Permanent resident & migrant	Freshwater & wetlands
___ Blue-winged teal	Summer resident	Freshwater
___ Cinnamon teal	Primarily summer resident	Ponds & marshes
___ European wigeon	Rare migrant	Wetlands & waterways
___ American wigeon	Permanent resident & migrant	Wetlands & waterways
___ Northern shoveler	Permanent resident & migrant	Marshes & sloughs

53

___ Wood duck	Rare resident	Rivers & ponds
___ Redhead	Permanent resident & migrant	Lakes & marshes
___ Canvasback	Permanent resident & migrant	Marshes & lakes
___ Greater scaup	Accidental	Marshes & lakes
___ Lesser scaup	Permanent resident & migrant	Freshwater
___ Common goldeneye	Winter resident	Lakes & rivers
___ Barrow's goldeneye	Rare winter resident	Rivers & waterways
___ Bufflehead	Uncommon resident & migrant	Freshwater
___ Oldsquaw	Rare winter visitor	Lakes & ponds
___ White-winged scoter	Accidental	Lakes
___ Surf scoter	Accidental	Lakes
___ Ruddy duck	Permanent resident & migrant	Marshes, ponds, & lakes
___ Hooded merganser	Migrant & winter resident	Ponds & rivers
___ Common merganser	Permanent resident	Streams & lakes
___ Red-breasted merganser	Accidental	Lakes

CATHARTIDAE (American Vultures)

___ Turkey vulture	Summer resident	Widely distributed

ACCIPITRIDAE (Hawks, Kites, Harriers, and Eagles)

___ White-tailed kite	Accidental	Fields & woodlands
___ Goshawk	Permanent resident & migrant	Forests & widely distributed
___ Sharp-shinned hawk	Rare resident	Forests & widely distributed
___ Cooper's hawk	Rare resident	Woodlands
___ Red-tailed hawk	Permanent resident	Widely distributed

___ Red-shouldered hawk	Accidental	Woodlands
___ Swainson's hawk	Summer resident & migrant	Widely distributed
___ Rough-legged hawk	Winter resident	Fields & wetlands
___ Ferruginous hawk	Uncommon resident	Arid plains & rangelands
___ Golden eagle	Permanent resident	Widely distributed
___ Bald eagle	Winter visitor	Waterways
___ Marsh hawk	Permanent resident	Wetlands & fields

PANDIONIDAE *(Ospreys)*

___ Osprey	Migrant	Waterways

FALCONIDAE *(Falcons)*

___ Prairie falcon	Permanent endangered resident	Widely distributed
___ Peregrine falcon	Rare endangered resident	Open country & mountain rimrocks
___ Merlin	Uncommon migrant	Marshes & open country
___ American kestrel	Permanent resident	Widely distributed

TETRAONIDAE *(Grouse)*

___ Blue grouse	Permanent resident	Forests
___ Ruffed grouse	Permanent resident	Primarily wooded bottom land
___ Sage grouse	Permanent resident	Sagebrush uplands

PHASIANIDAE *(Quail, Partridges, and Pheasants)*

___ California quail	Permanent resident	Streamside, thickets, & foothills
___ Mountain quail	Uncommon resident	Foothills & brushland
___ Ring-necked pheasant	Permanent resident	Well-watered uplands
___ Chukar	Permanent resident	Rocky slopes & canyons
___ Gray partridge	Rare resident	Foothills & grainfields

GRUIDAE *(Cranes)*

____ Sandhill Crane — Summer resident & migrant — Marshes, meadows, & fields

RALLIDAE *(Rails, Gallinules, and Coots)*

____ Virginia Rail	Permanent resident	Marshes
____ Sora	Permanent resident	Marshes & meadows
____ Common Gallinule	Accidental	Marshes & ponds
____ American Coot	Permanent resident	Freshwater & meadows

CHARADRIIDAE *(Plovers)*

____ Semipalmated plover	Rare migrant	Shorelines
____ Snowy plover	Summer resident	Alkali flats
____ Killdeer	Permanent resident	Widely distributed
____ American golden plover	Accidental	Shores & mudflats
____ Black-bellied plover	Uncommon migrant	Shorelines & marshes

SCOLOPACIDAE *(Snipes, Sandpipers, and other Shorebirds)*

____ Ruddy turnstone	Accidental	Mudflats
____ Common snipe	Permanent resident	Wetlands & waterways
____ Long-billed curlew	Summer resident	Fields & uplands
____ Whimbrel	Accidental	Fields & wetlands
____ Upland sandpiper	Accidental	Mountain valleys
____ Spotted sandpiper	Summer resident	Shores & streamside
____ Solitary sandpiper	Uncommon migrant	Wetlands
____ Willet	Summer resident	Marshes & meadows
____ Greater yellowlegs	Migrant	Marshes & waterways
____ Lesser yellowlegs	Migrant	Marshes & waterways

___ Red knot	Accidental	Mudflats & shores
___ Pectoral sandpiper	Migrant	Mudflats & shores
___ Baird's sandpiper	Rare migrant	Mudflats & shores
___ Least sandpiper	Migrant	Mudflats & shores
___ Dunlin	Migrant	Mudflats & shores
___ Sanderling	Accidental	Mudflats & shores
___ Long-billed dowitcher	Migrant	Mudflats & shores
___ Western sandpiper	Common migrant	Mudflats & shores
___ Marbled godwit	Migrant	Shores & pools

RECURVIROSTRIDAE (Avocets and Stilts)

___ American Avocet	Summer resident	Marshes, ponds, & mudflats
___ Black-necked stilt	Summer resident	Shallow lakes & marshes

PHALAROPODIDAE (Phalaropes)

___ Wilson's phalarope	Summer resident	Shores & shallow water
___ Red phalarope	Accidental	Lakes, ponds, & mudflats
___ Northern phalarope	Migrant	Lakes, ponds, & mudflats

STERCORARIIDAE

___ Parasitic jaeger	Accidental	Lakes

LARIDAE (Gulls and Terns)

___ Herring gull	Accidental	Waterways
___ California gull	Summer resident & migrant	Lakes & wetlands
___ Ring-billed gull	Summer resident & migrant	Lakes & wetlands
___ Laughing gull	Hypothetical	Lakes & marshes

Species	Status	Habitat
___ Franklin's gull	Summer resident	Lakes & marshes
___ Bonaparte's gull	Uncommon migrant	Waterways & lakes
___ Sabine's gull	Accidental	Waterways & lakes
___ Common tern	Accidental	Waterways
___ Forster's tern	Summer resident	Marshes & wetlands
___ Caspian tern	Migrant	Marshes & lakes
___ Black tern	Summer resident	Marshes & waterways

COLUMBIDAE *(Pigeons and Doves)*

Species	Status	Habitat
___ Band-tailed pigeon	Rare	Temporary visitor
___ Rock dove	Permanent resident	Cliffs & settlements
___ Mourning dove	Primarily summer resident	Widely distributed

CUCULIDAE *(Cuckoos)*

Species	Status	Habitat
___ Yellow-billed cuckoo	Accidental	Streamside vegetation

TYTONIDAE *(Barn Owls)*

Species	Status	Habitat
___ Barn Owl	Uncommon resident	Widely distributed

STRIGIDAE *(Owls)*

Species	Status	Habitat
___ Snowy owl	Rare winter resident	Open areas & shrub
___ Screech owl	Permanent resident	Wooded areas
___ Flammulated owl	Rare migrant	Wooded areas
___ Great horned owl	Permanent resident	Widely distributed
___ Pygmy owl	Permanent resident	Open woods
___ Burrowing owl	Summer resident	Open range & desert

___ Great gray owl	Rare permanent resident	Forests & meadows
___ Long-eared owl	Permanent resident	Wooded areas
___ Short-eared owl	Permanent resident	Marshes & meadows
___ Saw-whet owl	Rare permanent resident	Wooded areas

CAPRIMULGIDAE *(Poor-wills and Nighthawks)*

___ Poor-will	Summer resident—hibernates	Open juniper & sage
___ Common nighthawk	Summer resident	Widely distributed

APODIDAE *(Swifts)*

___ Vaux's swift	Summer resident	Forests & open sky
___ White-throated swift	Summer resident	Dry mountains & canyons

TROCHILIDAE *(Hummingbirds)*

___ Black-chinned hummingbird	Rare summer resident	Widely distributed
___ Broad-tailed hummingbird	Rare summer resident	Mountain meadows & thickets
___ Rufous hummingbird	Summer resident & migrant	Widely distributed
___ Calliope hummingbird	Summer resident	Forests

ALCEDINIDAE *(Kingfishers)*

___ Belted kingfisher	Permanent resident	Waterways

PICIDAE *(Woodpeckers)*

___ Common flicker	Permanent resident	Widely distributed
___ Pileated woodpecker	Permanent resident	Evergreen forests
___ Lewis' woodpecker	Permanent resident	Open forests & streamside

___ Yellow-bellied sapsucker	Permanent resident	Woodlands
___ Williamson's sapsucker	Summer resident	Forests & woodlands
___ Hairy woodpecker	Permanent resident	Forests & woodlands
___ Downy woodpecker	Permanent resident	Woodlands, streamside, & shade trees
___ White-headed woodpecker	Permanent resident	Pine & fir forests
___ Black-backed three-toed woodpecker	Permanent resident	Boreal forests
___ Northern three-toed woodpecker	Permanent resident	Boreal forests

TYRANNIDAE *(Flycatchers)*

___ Eastern kingbird	Summer resident	Widely distributed
___ Western kingbird	Summer resident	Widely distributed
___ Scissor-tailed flycatcher	Accidental	Semi-open areas
___ Ash-throated flycatcher	Summer resident	Juniper & desert shrub
___ Say's phoebe	Principally summer resident	Deserts, canyons, & settlements
___ Willow flycatcher	Summer resident	Streamside thickets
___ Hammond's flycatcher	Migrant & summer resident	Coniferous forests
___ Dusky flycatcher	Summer resident	Mountain shrub & woodlands
___ Gray flycatcher	Summer resident	Sagebrush & juniper
___ Western flycatcher	Migrant	Woodland & forests
___ Eastern wood pewee	Accidental	Woodlands
___ Western wood pewee	Summer resident	Woodlands, conifers, & streamside
___ Olive-sided flycatcher	Summer resident	Evergreen forests

60

ALAUDIDAE (*Larks*)

___ Horned lark	Permanent resident	Open areas

HIRUNDINIDAE (*Swallows*)

___ Violet-green swallow	Summer resident	Woodland & rimrocks
___ Tree swallow	Summer resident	Wide spread near trees & water
___ Bank swallow	Summer resident	Wide spread near banks & waterways
___ Rough-winged swallow	Summer resident	Near water
___ Barn swallow	Summer resident	Near water & human settlements
___ Cliff swallow	Summer resident	Cliffs & buildings near water
___ Purple martin	Rare summer resident	Open forests

CORVIDAE (*Jays, Magpies, and Crows*)

___ Gray jay	Permanent resident	Evergreen forests
___ Blue jay	Accidental	Woodlands
___ Steller's jay	Permanent resident	Evergreen forests
___ Scrub jay	Permanent resident	Juniper & scrub
___ Black-billed magpie	Permanent resident	Widely distributed
___ Common raven	Permanent resident	Widely distributed
___ Common crow	Permanent resident	Farmland & streamside
___ Piñon jay	Permanent resident	Juniper & sage
___ Clark's nutcracker	Permanent resident	Alpine areas & evergreen forests

PARIDAE (*Chickadees and Relatives*)

___ Black-capped chickadee	Permanent resident	Woods & thickets
___ Mountain chickadee	Permanent resident	Evergreen forests
___ Plain titmouse	Permanent resident	Juniper & streamside

____ Bushtit	Permanent resident	Juniper & streamside
SITTIDAE *(Nuthatches)*		
____ White-breasted nuthatch	Permanent resident	Forests & streamside
____ Red-breasted nuthatch	Permanent resident	Evergreens & woodlands
____ Pygmy nuthatch	Permanent resident	Pine forests
CERTHIIDAE *(Creepers)*		
____ Brown creeper	Permanent resident	Forests
CINCLIDAE *(Dippers)*		
____ Dipper	Permanent resident	Swift mountain streams
TROGLODYTIDAE *(Wrens)*		
____ House wren	Summer resident	Thickets & open woods
____ Winter wren	Permanent resident	Evergreen forests
____ Bewick's wren	Permanent resident	Thickets & juniper
____ Long-billed marsh wren	Permanent resident	Cattail & bulrush marsh
____ Cañon wren	Permanent resident	Cliffs & canyons
____ Rock wren	Permanent resident	Rocky areas
MIMIDAE *(Mockingbirds and Thrashers)*		
____ Mockingbird	Rare summer resident & migrant	Streamside & woodlands
____ Gray catbird	Rare summer resident	Undergrowth & brush
____ Brown thrasher	Accidental	Brushy thickets
____ Sage thrasher	Mainly summer resident	Desert scrub & thickets
TURDIDAE *(Thrushes, Bluebirds, and Solitaires)*		
____ American robin	Permanent resident	Widely distributed

___ Varied thrush	Summer resident	Evergreen forests & woodlands
___ Hermit thrush	Summer resident	Evergreen forests & woodlands
___ Swainson's thrush	Summer resident	Thickets & forests
___ Veery	Rare summer resident & migrant	Woodlands & streamside
___ Western bluebird	Permanent resident	Woodlands
___ Mountain bluebird	Permanent resident	Woodlands & open areas
___ Townsend's solitaire	Permanent resident	Forest; widely distributed

SYLVIIDAE *(Gnatcatchers and Kinglets)*

___ Blue-gray gnatcatcher	Rare summer resident	Junipers & thickets
___ Golden-crowned kinglet	Permanent resident	Forests & woodlands
___ Ruby-crowned kinglet	Permanent resident	Evergreen forests & woodlands

MOTACILLIDAE *(Pipits)*

___ Water pipit	Permanent resident	Alpine areas & near water

BOMBYCILLIDAE *(Waxwings)*

___ Bohemian waxwing	Migrant	Streamside & groves
___ Cedar waxwing	Permanent resident	Woodlands & shade trees

PTILOGONATIDAE *(Silky Flycatchers)*

___ Phainopepla	Accidental	Desert scrub

LANIIDAE *(Shrikes)*

___ Northern shrike	Winter resident	Open country
___ Loggerhead shrike	Permanent resident	Open country

STURNIDAE *(Starlings)*

___ Starling	Permanent resident	Widely distributed

VIREONIDAE *(Vireos)*

____ Hutton's vireo	Accidental	Woodlands
____ Solitary vireo	Summer resident	Mixed forests
____ Red-eyed vireo	Rare summer resident & migrant	Woodlands & shade trees
____ Warbling vireo	Summer resident	Aspen, streamside, & shade trees

PARULIDAE *(Wood Warblers)*

____ Black-and-white warbler	Accidental	Woodlands
____ Tennessee warbler	Accidental	Woodlands
____ Orange-crowned warbler	Summer resident	Aspen & brushy woodlands
____ Nashville warbler	Migrant (summer resident)	Woodlands & forest edges
____ Northern parula	Accidental	Moist woodlands
____ Yellow warbler	Summer resident	Streamside & shade trees
____ Black-throated blue warbler	Rare migrant	Woodlands
____ Cape May warbler	Accidental	Woods
____ Yellow-rumped warbler	Summer resident	Evergreen forests & woodlands
____ Black-throated gray warbler	Summer resident	Junipers & woodlands
____ Townsend's warbler	Migrant	Forests & woodlands
____ Black-throated green warbler	Accidental	Forests
____ Hermit warbler	Accidental	Woodlands
____ Chestnut-sided warbler	Accidental	Shrubs & shade trees
____ Bay-breasted warbler	Accidental	Woodlands
____ Blackpoll warbler	Accidental	Trees
____ Palm warbler	Accidental	Low trees & bushes
____ Ovenbird	Accidental	Woods & thickets
____ Northern waterthrush	Uncommon migrant	Moist woods & streamside

_____ MacGillivray's warbler — Summer resident — Undergrowth & thickets
_____ Common yellowthroat — Summer resident — Swamps, marshes, & streamside
_____ Yellow-breasted chat — Summer resident — Streamside thickets
_____ Wilson's warbler — Summer resident — Streamside thickets & woods
_____ American redstart — Uncommon summer res. & migrant — Streamside woodlands

PLOCEIDAE (*Weaver Finches*)

_____ House sparrow — Permanent resident — Near human settlements

ICTERIDAE (*Meadowlarks, Blackbirds, and Orioles*)

_____ Bobolink — Summer resident — Meadows
_____ Western meadowlark — Primarily summer resident — Open fields & meadows
_____ Yellow-headed blackbird — Primarily summer resident — Marshes & open country
_____ Red-winged blackbird — Permanent resident — Marshes, swamps, & fields
_____ Hooded oriole — Accidental — Woodlands
_____ Northern oriole — Summer resident — Streamside & shade trees
_____ Common grackle — Accidental — Lawns & shade trees
_____ Brewer's blackbird — Permanent resident — Widely distributed
_____ Brown-headed cowbird — Summer resident — Fields & open country

THRAUPIDAE (*Tanagers*)

_____ Western tanager — Summer resident — Forests & woodlands
_____ Summer tanager — Accidental — Stream bottoms

FRINGILLIDAE (*Grosbeaks, Finches, Sparrows, and Buntings*)

_____ Rose-breasted grosbeak — Accidental — Woodlands
_____ Black-headed grosbeak — Summer resident — Woodlands & streamside

___ Indigo bunting	Accidental	Brushy areas
___ Lazuli bunting	Summer resident	Sagebrush & streamside
___ Painted bunting	Accidental	Roadside & brushy areas
___ Evening grosbeak	Permanent resident	Coniferous forests & woodlands
___ Purple finch	Accidental	Woodlands
___ Cassin's finch	Permanent resident	High mountain forests
___ House finch	Mainly summer resident	Widely distributed
___ Pine grosbeak	Winter resident	Woodlands
___ Gray-crowned rosy finch	Permanent resident	Alpine areas
___ Black rosy finch	Summer resident	Crest of the Steens Mountain
___ Common redpoll	Rare winter resident	Brushy areas
___ Pine siskin	Summer resident	Evergreen forests & streamside
___ American goldfinch	Summer resident	Streamside & thickets
___ Lesser goldfinch	Migrant & summer resident	Streamside & brushy areas
___ Red crossbill	Permanent resident	Evergreen forests
___ Green-tailed towhee	Summer resident	Brushy slopes & canyons
___ Rufous-sided towhee	Primarily summer resident	Brush & streamside
___ Savannah sparrow	Summer resident	Watered, open areas
___ Vesper sparrow	Primarily summer resident	Open areas & sage
___ Lark sparrow	Summer resident	Open, brushy areas
___ Black-throated sparrow	Summer resident	Desert scrub
___ Sage sparrow	Summer resident	Sagebrush & desert
___ Dark-eyed junco	Permanent resident	Widely distributed
___ Gray-headed junco	Accidental	Forests & woodlands

Bird	Status	Habitat
___ Tree sparrow	Winter resident	Roadsides & weedy areas
___ Chipping sparrow	Summer resident	Widely distributed
___ Clay-colored sparrow	Accidental	Brushy areas
___ Brewer's sparrow	Summer resident	Sagebrush & weedy areas
___ Harris' sparrow	Uncommon winter resident	Brush & woodlands
___ White-crowned sparrow	Permanent resident	Widely distributed
___ Golden-crowned sparrow	Migrant	High mountains & brushy areas
___ White-throated sparrow	Uncommon migrant	Woodlands & thickets
___ Fox sparrow	Summer resident	Woodlands & brushy areas
___ Lincoln sparrow	Summer resident	High mountains, woodlands, & thickets
___ Song sparrow	Permanent resident	Thickets, marshes, & roadsides
___ Snow bunting	Uncommon winter resident	Fields & weedy areas

Oregon.

Probably because of the abundance of rodents and rabbits, many hawks live in the northern Great Basin. Red-tailed hawks and marsh hawks are numerous in the summer; rough-legged hawks and marsh hawks in the winter. Several other species are seen less frequently.

Golden eagles nest in lava rims throughout the desert region and hunt above vast expanses of rangelands and valleys. A nest near Narrows has been used almost continuously since 1882; two young were produced there in 1976. Jackrabbits are the staple food of golden eagles. Bald eagles winter in the northern Great Basin and accompany and feed on the great spring migrations of pintails as they move northward.

As early as February, sage grouse cocks gather before sunrise on tribal strutting grounds (leks) to commence their annual mating extravaganza. Until mid-May they appear each morning, take positions on a designated plot of ground, fan their tails, arch their wings, inflate air sacs, and strut their hearts out for seemingly unimpressed females. Accompanying the ritual is a sound that reminds one of water "popping" as it escapes down a drain. Most females mate with the single dominant male, and the entire male population is quite emaciated when the strutting season finally ends. Foster Flat and Hart Mountain are good places to observe the sage grouse dance. Sage grouse feed primarily on sagebrush leaves. The species is a tasty game bird and is hunted during a short season.

Visitor questionnaires reveal that sandhill cranes are the greatest biological attraction at Malheur Refuge. These magnificent birds stand four feet tall and seemingly fly with effortless grace—neck and legs fully extended. About 235 pairs of sandhills nest at Malheur, with smaller populations in other well-watered valleys (e.g., Alvord, Warner, etc.). In February cranes begin arriving; thousands of lesser sandhills that will continue northward to nest and greater sandhills, many of which remain. The same nesting territories are used year after year by the same pairs. Although two eggs are usually laid, normally only one chick is reared. When the trumpeting and varied calls of sandhills are heard, spring and the crane watchers can't be far behind.

Few places have a greater diversity of spectacular shorebirds than does the basin region. Long-billed curlews, willets, avocets, and black-necked stilts dot the meadows and flutter overhead. The melting snows of highlands make Great Basin valleys a paradise for these species.

Although there are many kinds of owls in the northern Great

Basin, the burrowing owl seems best to represent the area. Small and perched atop long legs, this peculiar owl appropriates an abandoned rodent burrow for its nesting site. After the young are able, they come out and stand around the burrow entrance, resembling an impromptu conference of mobsters as they wait for the parents to fetch small rodents or lizards. Great horned owls, often seen roosting in willow thickets by day, can thrill visitors just by batting their immense yellow eyes. Hearing the eerie hoot of a great horned owl is one of the most exciting experiences to be had in the high desert.

One of the last birds to arrive each spring (usually around May 25) is the common nighthawk. Attracted by the great hatches of aquatic insects, nighthawks fill the sky as they swoop and dart for food. They are notable for their precipitous diving, which produces a drag or fluttering of wing feathers and results in a characteristic drawn-out "burp". Many hear it, but few identify the source of the sound. Nighthawks can be seen roosting on all sorts of ridiculous perches (e.g., utility lines, rail fences, pipes, etc.)—always parallel to the roost—rather than across it.

Although belted kingfishers are widely distributed, they seem more visible in semi-arid areas, perhaps because they must hunt from utility lines and telephone poles, fence posts, and other conspicuous tree substitutes. Their rattling call and reckless plunges bring joy to many. Unfortunately, some fishermen assume that every fish caught by a kingfisher is a trout—an assumption that is quite incorrect.

Cliff swallows are perhaps the most visible summer bird in large areas of the northern Great Basin. Great swarming colonies nest on cliffs, bridges, and buildings, where they build their globular nests of mud, leaving only a small hole for entry. Barn swallows, which build a half-cup plastered to a vertical surface, usually nest inside culverts, under bridges, or in buildings. All swallows are valuable agents in controlling insects, and one wonders whether mosquitoes might become intolerable, were it not for the appetites and industry of swallows.

Dressed in an incongruent garb of white and black with an ungainly tail that seems aerodynamically ridiculous, the black-billed magpie seems to be the clown of the desert. But don't believe it! This conspicuous opportunist is a genius at survival—feeding on almost anything imaginable, hiding what can't be eaten at the moment, and exercising an uncanny alertness. Magpies have been despised (probably unfairly) and widely persecuted, but seem to thrive on adversity. When everyone else starves in the desert, the magpie will still be there laughing and picking clean the bones.

A gray flash erupting from a rushing mountain stream or a stubby dull-colored songster bobbing on a rock introduces the dipper to its new fans. After all, one can only admire a character who is willing to walk *underwater* in search of food. Dippers, too, have been accused of stealing the fisherman's trout (fishermen always have ready excuses), but if it is true, we say more power to the dipper. They feed primarily on invertebrates.

Shrikes are famous (or infamous) for their custom of impaling small prey on barbs of fences or thorns—presumably a way of setting aside something for hard times. This behavior has earned them the name of "butcherbird". The shrikes are sharp-eyed hunters, often spotting insects, lizards, or other small animals from utility poles or lines, fences, or more natural perches. With a rapid wingbeat and swift maneuverability, these miniature predators are most effective. Their silhouette is a familiar one to all who visit the desert.

A discussion of birds of the northern Great Basin would hardly be complete without a word about blackbirds. The marshes and meadows of interior valleys become a frenzy of flight and scolding voices during the nesting season. Few birds are more protective of their territories, and blackbirds will readily attack cranes, eagles, or a neighbor with equal vehemence. Yellow-headed blackbirds usually nest over deeper water, leaving shallows and meadows to the red-winged blackbirds. Brewer's blackbirds are more apt to nest in still drier sites. In the fall great mixed flocks of pre-migratory blackbirds often contain thousands of birds, and they can strip a small grainfield in short order.

Reptiles:

Reptiles are exceptionally well-adapted for living in arid and semi-arid environments, as shown by the rich reptilian fauna in deserts of the Southwest. A dry impervious skin and shelled eggs (or live birth) reduce their dependence upon water. Also, many reptiles, especially lizards, are able to tolerate unusually high temperatures. All reptiles hibernate. In the northern Great Basin, there are 10 species of lizards (4 families) and 8 species of snakes (3 families).

Lizards are active during the day, and some species go about their normal routine even when temperatures are extreme. Most lizards are quick and extremely agile. Insects and other arthropods compose the bulk of the diet, but some larger lizards also prey upon smaller species of lizards. None needs surface water. Lizards found in the Great Basin region of Oregon are as follows: FAMILY IGUANIDAE (Iguanids). Collared lizard (*Crotaphytus collaris*), leopard lizard (*Crotaphytus wislizeni*), Western fence lizard

(*Sceloporus occidentalis*), sagebrush lizard (*Sceloporus gracio-sus*), side-blotched lizard (*Uta stansburiana*), desert horned lizard (*Phrynosoma platyrhinos*), short-horned lizard (*Phrynosoma douglassi*); FAMILY SCINCIDAE (Skinks). Western skink (*Eumeces skiltonianus*); FAMILY TEIIDAE (Teids). Western whiptail (*Cnemidophorus tigris*); FAMILY ANGUIDAE (Alligator Lizards); Northern alligator lizard (*Gerrhonotus coeruleus*).

Although most snakes are active during daylight hours, others are active at night or both day and night. The diet is usually varied, but includes small animals such as insects, amphibians, reptiles, birds, and mammals. Garter snakes seek most of their food in or near water. Snakes present in the area are: FAMILY BOIDAE (Boas). Rubber boa (*Charina bottae*); FAMILY COLUBRIDAE (Colubrids). Racer (*Coluber constrictor*), striped whipsnake (*Masticophis taeniatus*), gopher snake (*Pituophis melanoleucus*), common garter snake (*Thamnophis sirtalis*), Western terrestrial garter snake (*Thamnophis elegans*), night snake (*Hypsiglena torquata*); FAMILY VIPERIDAE (Pit Vipers). Western rattlesnake (*Crotalus viridis*).

Because of specific habitat requirements, most reptiles are not continuously distributed over large areas. Being inconspicuous, reptiles are seldom observed and tend to be ignored. Only the rattlesnake attracts the attention of most visitors.

In the winter, rattlesnakes hibernate in dens, usually in crevices, boulder piles, rock slides, and similar retreats. In Utah 930 rattlers were captured at a single den during a 9-year study. Racers, striped whipsnakes, and gopher snakes commonly share rattlesnakes dens. When outdoor temperatures rise above 70°F (about 60°F inside the den), rattlesnakes emerge and bask in the sun near the den's entrance. At this time, the snakes are vulnerable, to the extent that 139 rattlers have been killed in a single day near a den.

After emerging, the snakes mate and leave the den for the summer. Breeding occurs when rattlesnakes reach 3 or 4 years of age. Living young are born about September, and the number of young ranges from 3 to 13, with 8 being average. The young are 11 or 12 inches at birth; adults may reach 4 feet, but seldom exceed 3 feet.

Rattlesnakes feed mainly on small rodents, but also take rabbits, birds, lizards, and other animals. Prey is killed by venom injected through a pair of hollow fangs which are normally folded back, but pop up when the mouth is opened. Temperature sensitive pits between the eyes and nostrils help locate warm-blooded prey.

Rattlesnakes are born with a single rattle or button and add a new rattle each time the skin is shed. Wild snakes often have four rattles after a year, six or seven after two years, but gain new rattles more slowly thereafter—usually at a rate of about one per year. Young captives given abundant food may grow seven to nine rattles a year. Carnival folks sometimes glue several sets of rattles on a single snake to impress customers. Many snake bites result from attempts to cut the rattle off a supposedly dead snake!

Many people feel terrorized by rattlesnakes. Actually, both stinging insects and lightning cause more deaths than rattlesnakes. Many visitors to the high desert worry about rattlesnakes, but driving a car to reach the desert is several thousand times more risky than the danger of snake bite after one arrives.

Amphibians:

The amphibians, with their moist skins and aquatic breeding and larval stages, are poorly adapted to the desert, and few species are to be found there.

Only one species of salamander, the long-toed salamander (*Ambystoma macrodactylum*—FAMILY AMBYSTOMATIDAE) occurs, principally in forested areas near the northern edge of the Great Basin. There are five species of frogs (four families) as follows: FAMILY PELOBATIDAE. Great Basin spadefoot (*Scaphiopus intermontanus*); FAMILY BUFONIDAE. Western toad (*Bufo boreas*); FAMILY HYLIDAE. Pacific treefrog (*Hyla regilla*); FAMILY RANIDAE. Spotted frog (*Rana pretiosa*) and bullfrog (*Rana catesbeiana*).

Spadefoots have huge eyes, vertical pupils, and special spades or digging devices on the hind feet. They are nocturnal and breed in permanent water or temporary pools formed by spring rains, at which time large numbers may be seen crossing highways. Both egg and larval stages are brief. During the daytime, especially in dry weather, adults burrow, using the spades and hind feet to dig backwards into loose soil or sand. They may come out at night to catch insects near lights.

Fishes:

In the northern Great Basin are 41 species of fishes belonging to 9 families. (Table 3). The composition and distribution of the fish fauna reflect several important ecological and historical factors. Because of internal drainage, many species are unable to gain entry into the basin area—especially anadromous fishes such as salmon. Other currently landlocked species obviously reached the basin when outlets to nearby rivers did exist (e.g., the Harney Basin once drained into the Malheur River system, and Goose Lake originally drained into the Pit River).

Table 3. A list of fishes found in the northern Great Basin, including Goose Lake, but excluding the Klamath Basin.

Family and Name	Distribution, habitat, etc.
PETROMYZONTIDAE *(Lampreys)*	
Pacific lamprey *(Lampetra tridentata)*	Goose Lake-landlocked
Pit-Klamath brook lamprey *(Lampetra lethophaga)*	Goose Lake-landlocked
SALMONIDAE *(Trout and relatives)*	
Kokanee *(Oncorhynchus nerka)*	Yellowjacket Lake - introduced
Brown trout *(Salmo trutta)*	McDermitt Creek - introduced
Redband trout *(Salmo sp.)*	Widely distributed - streams
Cutthroat trout *(Salmo clarki)*	Alvord Basin drainages
Rainbow trout *(Salmo gairdneri)*	Native and widely introduced
Brook trout *(Salvelinus fontinalis)*	Introduced - Fish Lake drainage
Mountain whitefish *(Prosopium williamsoni)*	Harney Basin, streams
CYPRINIDAE *(Minnows)*	
Carp *(Cyprinus carpio)*	Harney Basin - introduced
Tui chub *(Gila bicolor)*	Widely distributed, lakes
Alvord chub *(Gila alvordensis)*	Locally in Alvord Basin
Redside shiner *(Richardsonius balteatus)*	Harney Basin
Lahontan redside *(Richardsonius egregius)*	Lahontan Basin
Northern squawfish *(Ptychocheilus oregonensis)*	Northern Harney Basin

73

California roach (*Hesperoleucus symmetricus*)   Goose Lake drainage
Chiselmouth (*Acrocheilus alutaceus*)   Northern Harney Basin
Speckled dace (*Rhinichthys osculus*)   Widely distributed
Longnose dace (*Rhinichthys cataractae*)   Northern Harney Basin

CATOSTOMIDAE (Suckers)

Largescale sucker (*Catostomus macrocheilus*)   Harney Basin
Sacramento sucker (*Catostomus occidentalis*)   Goose Lake drainage
Warner sucker (*Catostomus warnerensis*)   Warner Valley
Tahoe sucker (*Catostomus tahoensis*)   Lahontan Basin
Mountain sucker (*Catostomus platyrhynchus*)   Lahontan Basin
Bridgelip sucker (*Catostomus columbianus*)   Harney Basin

ICTALURIDAE (*Catfish - Introduced*)

Channel catfish (*Ictalurus punctatus*)   Harney Basin?
Yellow bullhead (*Ictalurus natalis*)   Warner Valley
Black bullhead (*Ictalurus melas*)   Warner Valley
Brown bullhead (*Ictalurus nebulosus*)   Warner Valley
Flathead catfish (*Pylodictis olivaris*)   Moon Reservoir?

POECILIIDAE (*Livebearers - Introduced*)

Mosquitofish (*Gambusia affinis*)   Virgin Springs, Nevada

CENTRARCHIDAE *(Sunfishes - Introduced)*

Smallmouth bass *(Micropterus dolomieui)*	Northern Malheur Basin
Largemouth bass *(Micropterus salmoides)*	Widely introduced
Pumpkinseed *(Lepomis gibbosus)*	Widely introduced
Bluegill *(Lepomis macrochirus)*	Widely introduced
Black crappie *(Pomoxis nigromaculatus)*	Sparingly introduced
White crappie *(Pomoxis annularis)*	Widely introduced

PERCIDAE *(Perch - Introduced)*

Yellow perch *(Perca flavenscens)*	Widely introduced

COTTIDAE *(Sculpins)*

Mottled sculpin *(Cottus bairdi)*	Harney Basin
Pit sculpin *(Cottus pitensis)*	Goose Lake drainage?
Torrent sculpin *(Cottus rhotheus)*	Fish Lake - introduced

Many basin streams originate at high elevations where they are rocky, cold, swift, and well-aerated. At lower elevations the same streams may become warmer and sluggish, with bottoms of sand or mud. Some streams even disappear before reaching a basin. Large springs may form a surface flow, only to disappear again into the ground. Differences in temperature, alkalinity, rainfall, and evaporation also strongly influence distribution. Human introduction, accidental and purposeful, have further complicated matters.

Several species and subspecies in the northern Great Basin region are endangered or threatened, and others are probably in need of protection. The Malheur sculpin and Pit sculpin are apparently extinct.

The area has not been exhaustively studied, and fishes new to science may await discovery. The redband trout is an undescribed species, as is the Alvord cutthroat, which occurs in certain streams in the Trout Creek Mountains. The Alvord chub was not described until 1972.

Invertebrates:

It is beyond the province of this book to deal with the various groups of invertebrates. However, we would be negligent not to point out that a rich invertebrate fauna exists in the high desert area. Interesting aquatic groups include fairy shrimp, tadpole shrimp, a great many kinds of colorful dragon and damsel flies, fantastic hatches of may flies, and large numbers of hungry and persistent mosquitoes.

Some interesting and conspicuous terrestrial invertebrates include Jerusalem crickets, harvester ants, cicadas, numerous gall insects (especially on sagebrush), bombadier beetles, scorpions, and a large selection of butterflies.

Paleontology:

About 35 million years ago, a strange and primitive assemblage of animals inhabited eastern Oregon. Some typical groups included uintatheres, titanotheres, chalicotheres, tiny four-toed horses, several kinds of rhinoceroses, oreodonts, tapirs, and crocodiles. By 20 million years ago, numerous others were present, including various dog and bear-like forms, saber tooth tigers, ancestral weasels and raccoons, rodents, lagomorphs, elephant relatives, antelopes, camels, peccaries, various deer, and more advanced types of rhinoceroses and horses.

In the Pliocene, with the formation of major mountain ranges, the interior began drying. As a result, some ancient mammals (e.g., oreodonts and rhinoceroses) disappeared, tapirs and camels began to decline, and plains-dwelling types such as horses and antelope increased. Certain South American groups, such as ground sloths and glyptodonts, invaded the area at this time.

The ice ages and the long period of drying that followed brought about wholesale extinction. Dire wolves, saber tooth tigers, tapirs, horses, camels, several types of elephants, mastodons, ground sloths, and numerous others were victims.

Today the Great Basin fauna consists primarily of animals that have survived a long history of adaptation to semi-arid and arid environments. South American species, such as the porcupine, and numerous Old World groups (e.g., deer), which arrived by way of the Bering land bridge, are also represented. But, whatever their origins or history, Great Basin animals provide a rich and enjoyable experience for the many thousands of high desert visitors who come to see them.

CHAPTER 7

Adaptations to Arid Environments

In deserts temperatures are high, solar radiation is intense because of clear air and minimal cloud cover, and shade is scarce. Furthermore, low rainfall, scant surface water, low humidity, and dry winds prevail. Desert water and soil often contain excessive amounts of salts. Without water a person can survive only a day or two in a hot desert, although many kinds of smaller animals may live there permanently. How do living things cope, physically and behaviorally, with these conditions?

In this hostile environment of too much heat and too little water, an organism must keep its body temperature down while holding water loss to a minimum. Temperature and water problems are intimately and inseparably related, and organisms have evolved diverse adaptations for dealing with them. Because they can move, desert animals have a great advantage over plants; however, plants and animals frequently depend upon similar survival strategies. For example, both may resort to a state of dormancy to avoid the hottest and driest season. Other adaptations of desert organisms relate to wind, the absence of trees, and sandy soil. This chapter describes some behavioral and physiological adaptations of plants, animals, and humans living in deserts.

Plants:

Plants well adapted to live in arid or semi-arid environments are called xerophytes—literally "dry plants". Water balance is generally more critical to plants than is temperature regulation. Plants use three basic schemes to cope with water problems—escape, evasion, and endurance.

Some plants escape drought by completing growth and reproduction during the favorable part of the year, leaving seed (e.g., annuals such as cheatgrass) or bulbs (e.g., wild onions) to initiate growth the next year. A single halogeton, an introduced species, produces as many as 50,000 seeds of two types—about 65% germinate immediately or the next spring, and the rest, which have delayed germination, may remain viable 10 years or more.

Many desert perennials, such as budsage quickly grow and set seed in the spring and early summer, drop their leaves with the approach of the hot, dry season, and then become dormant until favorable conditions return—a process similar to estivation in some animals.

Xerophytes have numerous ways of restricting water loss and evading the consequences of water shortage. Although each adaptation may conserve water, none is sufficiently effective by itself, so many are likely to be found in an individual plant.

A thick cuticle or waxy layer may reduce water loss from leaf and stem surfaces. The wax layer may also scatter light and diminish ultraviolet penetration. Hairs, thorns, and spines can reduce water loss by blocking and reflecting solar radiation and creating a dead air space at the plant surface. Such a boundary layer of air insulates deeper tissues from extreme temperatures and reduces evaporative losses to the atmosphere. Plants may also conserve water by having fewer or sunken stomata, or by closing the stomata during the day and opening them only at night when the temperature is lower and humidity higher.

Succulent plants store water in leaves and reduce evaporation by bearing leaves with small surface areas in relation to volume. Many chenopods of the northern Great Basin, including greasewood, possess succulent leaves. Methods of reducing the exposure of leaf surface include size reduction, leaf rolling, shape modification, and a decrease in the number of leaves. Many desert plants drop some of their leaves as the dry season becomes severe, and many have photosynthetic stems with leaves modified for other functions.

Root systems may be modified in various ways to enable plants to reach water supplies. Succulent plants often have shallow, fibrous root systems which catch runoff from rains. These plants are able to quickly collect a large amount of surface water, store it, and survive drought until the next rains. Other plants send long tap roots down to the water table, often to depths exceeding 60 feet. Plants like greasewood, using the tap root to probe for ground water at great depths, are called phreatophytes—from the Greek *phreatos* which means "a well". Some species are equipped with both systems. Big sagebrush has most of its roots in the upper 2 feet of soil, but will send a tap root down 6 feet or more to reach permanent water.

Certain resistant succulents, such as cacti, are able to endure long periods of drought. In addition to storing water and having a shallow root system that can quickly accumulate large quantities of water, these plants frequently possess tissues and protoplasm that can tolerate extreme dehydration. Their enzyme systems may be exceedingly stable in the presence of high temperatures. Among the lower plants, some lichens can withstand temperatures above 158°F. Many cacti grow and orient in a manner to reduce exposure to maximum solar radiation.

Many plants in the Great Basin are halophytes—highly tolerant of salts. They may grow near playas and even in accumulations of salt. The roots of halophytes (e.g., greasewood, halogeton) are able to penetrate surface salt deposits and reach the water table. Because a crust of salt is a hostile site for seed germination, vegetative reproduction by underground runners (e.g., desert saltgrass) is an effective alternative to sexual reproduction. Some halophytes accumulate large amounts of salt in their tissues, thereby, creating a favorable osmotic gradient for uptake of water. Excess salts may be extruded by special glands (e.g., saltbushes), lost as leaves are shed during droughts (e.g., saltbushes and halogeton), or combined with other substances and stored in a state non-toxic to the plant. When leaf litter containing large amounts of salt accumulates around the base of a plant, the soil pH increases measurably and may exclude less salt-tolerant species.

Other adaptations of desert plants include thorns and spines that protect the plants against browsing animals. Accumulations of pungent chemicals may serve the same purpose. An entire plant being tumbled by winds, as in Russian thistle, is a particularly effective seed dispersal mechanism in windswept and open desert areas.

Animals:

Movement gives animals a distinct advantage in avoiding environmental extremes. When ambient temperatures are high, desert animals must rid themselves of heat produced internally during metabolism. Most environmental heat is picked up from processes of radiation, conduction, and convection. Animals maintaining a constant body temperature (e.g., birds and mammals) must cool themselves when the outside temperature exceeds body temperature. Desert animals have many adaptations for escaping, evading, or resisting adverse temperatures and water shortages.

Size is a critical factor in thermoregulation of animals. Small animals, having a large surface area relative to volume, heat up faster than larger animals in a hot environment. Small animals do not usually pant or sweat to cool themselves, but are able to hide in cool retreats, which are harder to come by for larger animals. Most desert animals are light colored, which helps reflect solar radiation and provides protective coloration. The presence of feathers and hairs insulates against heat gain and water loss by creating dead air spaces between the skin and atmosphere.

Animals obtain water from metabolism (i.e., oxidation of hydrogen to form metabolic water), from their food, and by drinking. Also, the Pacific treefrog and some insects extract water directly from humid air. Water is lost by evaporation from the skin and respiratory tract, and in urine, feces, and milk. All these pathways of gain and loss may be modified for water economy.

Many organisms escape the hostility of the desert by nesting or giving birth to young when temperatures are moderate and water more abundant. When the hot, dry season arrives, the young are self-sufficient, the adults are less encumbered by parental chores, and all individuals are free to modify their behavior to alleviate environmental stresses.

Estivation is an ideal means of escape. Unlike hibernation, which occurs at low temperatures, estivation happens when the weather is hot and dry. The estivating animal becomes torpid or dormant. Most estivators go underground, usually in a burrow, where the body temperature drops close to that of the surroundings. Rates of respiration, metabolism, and other physiological processes slow down and approach those of hibernation. In fact, many estivating animals enter hibernation without interruption. Belding ground squirrels at Malheur Refuge headquarters disappear in August and do not reappear until March. Essentially estivation gives the animal the benefits of cold-bloodedness, and by breathing cool, moist air and exhaling air that is not warmed in the body, estivating animals reduce evaporation and conserve water. Furthermore, the diminished metabolism makes it possible for the fat reserves to last longer. Whiptails and some insects estivate.

When animals are unable to escape the harshness of deserts, they may put up with it, but evade dire consequences through special behavioral patterns. Desert birds are usually active early in the morning and late in the afternoon, but remain inactive in the shade during the heat of the day. Many animals, big and small, are nocturnal, restricting their activity to hours when temperatures are low and humidities high; days are spent sleeping or resting in burrows, shade, or other protected retreats.

Burrowing, a characteristic of many nocturnal animals, is a particularly effective way of avoiding extreme air and surface temperatures. Because burrows are cool and contain humid air, they are ideally suited for desert rodents, most of which lack sweat glands, do not pant, and, being small, could not afford to use their limited water supplies for cooling anyway. Water loss per unit of exposed surface area is about the same in small and large animals, but small animals are more vulnerable because they have so little water to lose. Spadefoots may burrow for long periods, coming out infrequently to feed at night or after a rain. Some snakes and certain lizards and insects often spend the hottest part of the day buried in sand or temporarily housed in the burrow of another animal.

Posture is used in thermoregulation. A lizard emerging from its burrow or hiding place in the morning may at first expose its head to the sun. By heating the head, the lizard increases its metabolism and is able to move and respond more effectively when it emerges completely. Once exposed fully to the sun, the lizard orients its body so as to intercept as much solar radiation as possible. After the lizard warms to an optimum temperature, it continually changes positions to maintain that temperature. Later when the lizard becomes too hot, it moves to shade or even returns to the burrow. Thereafter, movement between shade and sunlight keeps the body temperature within the proper range. Lizards can also change color to increase or decrease the amount of absorbed solar radiation—blanching when hot and darkening when cool.

On a hot day, a jackrabbit's body temperature, respiration rate, and water loss from the body surface increase. They do not sweat and make no use of burrows. Because food (often dry) and metabolic water are the jackrabbit's principle sources of water, cooling without large expenditures of water is imperative. When in the sun, the jackrabbit orients its huge ears—a large surface area—to reduce exposure to solar radiation. In shade the ears, which are well supplied with blood vessels, serve as radiators and transfer large amounts of heat from the blood to the atmosphere—without loss of water.

Unlike most ground squirrels, the antelope ground squirrel is out and active on the hottest days. The undersurface of the tail is white, and when arched over the back, the tail becomes an effective reflecting surface and also shades much of the body. In addition to this unusual postural device, antelope ground squirrels have thick, insulating skins and frequently retire to the burrow where they cool themselves by resting in contact with the burrow walls. Some tenebrionid beetles have a method of cooling that is similar to the antelope ground squirrel's use of its tail. Between the elytra (the hard outer wing) and the body is an air space connected to the outside, thus allowing a pathway for escape of heated air.

Wild burros, originally domesticated, but now feral throughout most of the Great Basin, are unusual in being able to let their body temperature rise significantly during the day and then drop at night, thereby avoiding use of water for evaporative cooling. Although this physiological device would appear to offer a ready solution to problems of desert living, no animal uses it exclusively or well.

In the absence of surface water, many small rodents will drink from droplets of dew or selectively eat the leaves of succulent plants. Antelope ground squirrels increase the percentage of insects in their diet during extended dry spells. Contrary to popular belief, no animal is able to store water for long periods (as do the cacti).

Perhaps the most fascinating desert animals are those that can survive without drinking, those that subsist on metabolic water only. Kangaroo rats can survive for years without water, and prefer dry food, even when green food is available. Quail are also able to survive on metabolic water and water obtained in food.

Animals persisting largely on metabolic water are extremely stingy when it comes to relinquishing water stored in their bodies. Many of them have highly efficient kidneys and excrete concentrated urine containing only small amounts of water. Kangaroo rats can drink sea water, which is fatal to most animals, rid themselves of the excess salts, and retain most of the water. Also, many desert animals such as kangaroo rats and jackrabbits produce extremely dry feces, recovering most of the water before release.

The kidneys of birds and reptiles excrete uric acid—a salt—rather than urine, and are able to recover almost all of the water. With this efficient kidney, some species of birds, such as the Savannah sparrow, are also able to drink sea water.

Resisting an increase in body temperature by evaporative cooling is effective, but costly in terms of water losses and physiological disruptions. Panting (e.g., coyotes) removes internal heat when water is evaporated from the lungs, respiratory tract, mouth, and tongue. Unlike sweating, panting has the advantages of no accompanying salt loss and instant voluntary control of the rate of cooling. Even though most panting is shallow, it has the disadvantage of removing too much carbon dioxide from the blood and causing alkalosis. Because birds maintain higher body temperatures than mammals, they can release heat to the atmosphere at higher temperatures and delay evaporative cooling until the ambient temperature exceeds their high body temperature. Birds cool by panting—actually by throat fluttering, a shallow form of panting. Although lizards pant when hot, they are probably not cooling themselves, but increasing oxygen intake to meet the increased demand of a higher metabolism produced by the rise in body temperature.

Sweating, the usual form of cooling among large mammals, is effective but requires large amounts of water. Unfortunately, in deserts where profuse sweating may be necessary, water is scarce. A major disadvantage of sweating is that salts are lost along with the water. The amount of salt loss varies, and the sweat of some animals may be very dilute. Water lost in sweating may cause a reduction in the volume of blood plasma, increased viscosity of the blood, and stress upon the heart and circulatory system. Excessive sweating can be harmful to humans.

Animals that sweat must be able to tolerate drastic dehydration. Camels and donkeys can tolerate loss of about 30% of their body weight from sweating. The remarkable thing is that they can drink enough in a few minutes to replace these huge water deficits. Dogs, too, can replace large amounts of water in a single drinking, but man, as we shall see, cannot.

Many adaptations of animals in the northern Great Basin are unrelated or only indirectly related to temperature and water problems. Birds nesting at the base of a shrub will often place the nest on the windward side rather than the leeward side, so that winds will keep the nest free of dust and sand. In sandy areas, rodents dig burrows at the base of a plant where the root system provides support and prevents collapse of the burrow. The roots also deter digging predators such as coyotes and badgers.

Because of the vast expanse of treeless terrain, desert birds use many human structures as tree substitutes in nesting, roosting, and perching. Ravens nest on abandoned windmill platforms, kingbirds nest on utility poles, nighthawks roost on utility lines (and even cars), raptors hunt from utility poles, and an Eastern kingbird, near Princeton, built its nest in the mouth of a wind sock. One wonders what birds did before there were fence posts!

Most animals have a large number of adaptations for desert life and do not depend on just one or a few. Spadefoots are a good example. They burrow, are nocturnal, and can tolerate severe dehydration. When buried, spadefoots accumulate urea, thereby producing a favorable gradient to prevent water loss to the surrounding soil. Spadefoots have no definite breeding season, are stimulated to breed by heavy rainfall, breed in temporary pools, and have extremely loud voices that enable them to form large breeding assemblages rapidly. Egg and larval development are rapid, and the tadpoles, unlike those of most frogs, feed on both plant and animal foods—a protein diet contributing to rapid growth. Also, the tadpoles are extremely heat resistant and produce growth inhibitors that decrease the growth rate of any competing tadpoles. Although other adaptations could be mentioned, these illustrate the point.

Humans:

The heat, sun, aridity, lack of resources, and isolation of the desert can be attractions or formidable obstacles to humans—depending upon the circumstances. To cope with these factors, humans have some basic physiological adaptations, but under ordinary conditions, man is more likey to resort to technological, cultural, psychological, or social solutions.

A person can tolerate extremely high temperatures in dry air by resorting to sweating, reducing activity, or assuming a position about 2 feet above the ground while exposing maximum surface area to the atmosphere—in the shade if possible. We, too, must contend with both environmental and metabolic sources of heat.

A person's initial responses to extreme desert heat are intense sweating, a desire to discard clothing, thirst, nausea, and dizziness. Lips, eyes, and mucous membranes of the nasal chamber become dry. Small blood vessels in the skin dilate, which helps radiate heat to the environment, but diminishes blood supply to other vital areas (e.g., kidneys, brain, digestive organs, etc.). Urine production may drop to half. If a great deal of sweating occurs, the volume of blood plasma is reduced, the blood becomes more viscous, and the heart must work harder. Although the pulse rate increases, the volume of blood pumped per beat (stroke volume) decreases, thus the heart's output is little changed. All of these physiological changes produce a rise in body temperature and dehydration.

After 4 to 10 days of exposure to desert heat, especially with normal activity, a person becomes acclimated and may sweat more (10 to 20%), but the sweat is dilute and contains less salt. Blood volume may increase as much as 15%, the heart rate decreases, stroke volume increases, and more blood is shunted to the skin. Body temperature drops. The acclimated person tends to get thirstier, maintains a better salt balance, but shows no decrease in need for water.

For humans, water shortage is much more critical than heat. We cannot store water nor reduce our needs. At about 104°F a man must evaporate about 1.5% of his body weight per hour to maintain a constant body temperature. He can only replace that loss by drinking more liquid. On a hot day a person may sweat 0.5 to 1.7 liters per hour; under extreme experimental conditions, the rate may reach 4 liters per hour—an amazing loss when one considers that the total volume of blood contains only about 4 liters of water. Symptoms of dehydration include intense but temporary thirst after water loss equivalent to 2% of the body weight, a dry mouth, cessation of sweating, sluggishness, and irritability after 4% loss, and loss of equilibrium and sense of direction, cessation of salivary gland function, and difficulty swallowing after 8% loss. A 12% loss is usually fatal, but if potable liquid is available, recovery can be nearly complete an hour after drinking. If one drinks an excess of water, it will be excreted by the kidneys, usually in an hour or so, but can be used for cooling while it lasts. At a daytime temperature of 120°F, it takes nearly 4 liters per day for an adult to maintain water balance, even with minimal activity. The only way to reduce water needs is to reduce heat gain and slow the loss of body water.

Unlike many animals, man will not instinctively drink enough water to replace all his losses after suffering extreme dehydration—the sensation of thirst may be satisfied even though a deficiency of 2 to 5% of the body weight still exists. This deficit will probably not be made up until the first major meal, at which time additional liquids will be taken.

Sweat contains sodium, chloride, potassium, lesser amounts of other elements, lactic acid, and urea. Replacing water after extreme dehydration, without replacing salts, can cause problems. Normally an acclimated person, who is producing a dilute sweat, gets enough salt in the diet to meet bodily needs. Others may need salt tablets. It is not difficult to see why salt has a value equivalent to that of gold in some parts of the world.

Evaporation from respiration and sweating is the only physiological weapon a person has to combat intense solar radiation, heat reflection from terrain, hot winds, and high air temperatures. Because desert air is dry, sweat evaporates rapidly and leaves the skin dry. Strong, hot winds will increase evaporative cooling only to a point, after which they may heat the body by conduction—just as fans may aggravate rather than solve heat problems in a hot room. Activity increases production of metabolic heat, therefore one can cool by doing nothing or by doing only what is required with the least amount of effort—and preferably at night when temperatures are lower. Relaxed muscles reduce heat production; toned muscles produce heat, as in shivering.

In the desert, few of us are ever forced to rely on only our physiological mechanisms for survival—we seldom venture far without our technology—clothing, cars, canteens, and the like.

Besides providing the latest in style, clothes provide essential protection against the elements in desert areas. Clothes can cut water loss by one-third, reduce heat gain by reflecting and insulating, and protect against ultraviolet, which burns exposed skin and may cause skin cancer. If clothes are not to interfere with evaporation, they should be loose—unlike the typical garb of cowboys. Although white clothes reflect much visible light, they are a black body for infrared, which constitutes about half of the energy in solar radiation. And although light-weight clothing keeps out wind, it provides little protection against cool nights, when a person can die of heat loss in many desert areas. Short sleeves and shorts may be comfortable, but they are not good for water economy. Native desert people in various parts of the world wear heavy wool or mohair garments—loose enough to permit evaporation, but heavy enough to insulate during the day and provide warmth at night.

For those who live in the desert, such technological features as transportation, well drilling equipment, irrigation systems, and communications are essential. Desert houses are made more comfortable and economical by appropriate designs, uses of special materials, insulation, air conditioning, and proper use of glass, paints, and shade trees.

Psychological factors or attitudes strongly influence successful human adjustment to desert environments. Keeping calm, avoiding excitement and stress, exercising good judgement, accepting reality, reducing aggression, and increasing tolerance, while admirable and desirable elsewhere, can be a matter of life or death in the desert. Even these behaviors are all altered with even slight dehydration. Although experience obviously helps, preparation is more important.

Social and cultural practices can make life easier for desert people. Training and education were essential to native peoples who lived in the Great Basin. Today technology has largely replaced social and cultural considerations.

A man can cope with the desert if he has water, food, and good health. Although technology provides much security, one must still exert an extra effort to succeed in making a good living in arid regions. A catastrophic failure of the artificial life support system provided by technology causes more serious problems to people living in the desert today than in former times when life was simpler and people lived closer to Nature.

Rueb Long, who spent his life in the desert and was as close to being a desert philosopher as anyone is likely to be, had a ready formula for desert survival. He advised us to ride fast horses and breathe through our noses. Because a person can lose 12 liters of water a day in the desert, we would add that one should take along plenty of water—and perhaps a bottle opener!

CHAPTER 8

Resources and Economy

Chambers of Commerce are always on the lookout for a catchy phrase—one that might entice even the most phrase-wary tourist. The slogan "Big Country" has been chosen by the Harney County Chamber, and no one can quarrel with the validity of their choice—the Great Basin is indeed big country.

In Oregon, the Great Basin takes in most of Harney County, the state's largest (area 10,131 square miles, 6,483,840 acres), and most of Lake County (8,269 square miles, 5,292,160 acres). By contrast, Oregon's smallest county, Multnomah, contains only 423 square miles. Also included in the basin are small portions of Klamath, Deschutes, Crook, Grant, and Malheur counties. Harney County, slightly smaller than Maryland, is larger than eight of the states—Connecticut, Delaware, Hawaii, Massachusetts, New Hampshire, New Jersey, Rhode Island, and Vermont—and Harney and Lake counties combined are about half the size of Indiana. But to put matters in proper perspective, it should be pointed out that the true cash value of taxable property in Harney County in 1972 was only 99 million dollars—less than the cost of a single B-1 bomber.

More than half of Oregon (52%) is federally administered, and in the Great Basin region of Oregon, the federal agencies administer about 73% of all lands. In Harney County ownership is as follows: Bureau of Land Management 63.8%. U.S. Forest Service 7.9%, Bureau of Indian Affairs 0.2%, other federal agencies 2.8%, state 3.3%, and private 22%. Just the BLM holdings in Harney County (4,686,000 acres) exceed the total combined areas of Oregon's ten smallest counties (Benton, Clatsop, Columbia, Hood River, Lincoln, Multnomah, Polk, Sherman, Washington, and Yamhill). In Lake County the BLM holdings are smaller (49.3%), but U.S. Forest Service holdings are larger (19.3%). Hart Mountain National Antelope Refuge (275,000 acres) and Malheur National Wildlife Refuge (181,000 acres) have a combined area larger than six of Oregon's 36 counties.

In this century, Oregon's population has become increasingly concentrated west of the Cascades, particularly in the Willamette

Valley and metropolitan area of Portland. In 1910, 21% of the state's population was found in eastern Oregon, but by 1970 only 13% lived there, even though it includes 69% of the land area. The Great Basin area has a lower population density than other parts of the state. The 30th senate district, which includes seven eastern Oregon counties and is larger than 14 of the states, has only 75,000 people, but constitutes 41% of the state's areas. Harney County, with a population of 5,374 in 1940, had about 7,500 in 1976—a density of about 0.7 persons per square mile (less than 0.2 outside of Burns and Hines). In Lake County there were 6,293 people in 1940 and about 6,620 in 1976—a density of 0.8 per square mile. In these two counties there are 834 acres for every person, compared with 0.49 acres per person in Multnomah County.

Almost half the people living in Oregon's Great Basin country were born in another state. Among minority groups, people of Spanish speaking ancestry are most numerous (less than 5%), American Indians constitute just over 1%, and Chinese, Japanese, and Blacks are barely represented. Compared with the rest of Oregon, the Great Basin region tends to have a slight excess of males, fewer older people, and a small deficit in the 20-40 year-old age group.

Burns and Lakeview are the only incorporated towns of more than 2,500 people in the region. Hines, which is contiguous with Burns, Paisley, and Seneca are the only other incorporated towns. About 68% of Harney County's population lives within Burns and Hines. Most other settlements in the region consist of single businesses, usually combined general store, post office, and gas station, and occasionally a restaurant and a few motel units. Some examples are Silvies, Buchanan, Lawen, Crane, Princeton, Diamond, Frenchglen, Fields, Adel, Plush, Wagontire, Riley, Hampton, Brothers, and Millican. Because all of these places are on road maps (otherwise large sections of the map would be blank), many visitors expect more than they find. During the Bi-centennial year, a representative of a national bicycle tour wrote to Princeton and requested accommodations for several dozen bike riders. He also suggested that it might be appropriate for the mayor and other city dignitaries to arrange a proper ceremony to greet the bicycle convoy. Princeton consists of a single building—not counting a shed and two out-of-door toilets! McDermitt and Denio straddle the Nevada-Oregon state line, but are considered Nevada towns because of the locations of their post offices.

As we would expect in such a large and sparsely populated area, services of all kinds are minimal. Although major highways serve Burns and Lakeview, both being county seats, much of the region can be reached only by gravel roads, and in many instances, roads to remote areas are barely passable in ordinary passenger cars. Branch railroads serve Lakeview and Burns (a private railroad extends from Burns to Seneca), but there is no passenger service. These two communities have minimal bus service and airports. No commercial air service, other than charter flights was available until 1977, when flights connecting various eastern Oregon cities and Portland were initiated. Small airstrips are found widely scattered throughout the area. Other services available only in Lakeview and Burns include hospitals, radio stations, weekly newspapers, movie theaters, and many commercial and personal services. Burns, Hines, and Lakeview have cable television, and most of the outlying areas are serviced by translator stations. Lakeview, with fewer than 3,000 people, offers an unusual variety of services and is the largest business center, as measured by bank and savings deposits, in the area.

Electricity and telephone are the only utilities extending outside major settlements. Water, sewage, and garbage services are privately arranged in most areas outside incorporated towns. Fire and police protection are largely absent in rural areas.

Although grammar schools, often of the one-room variety, are located in several communities, there are only four high schools in the area (Burns, Lakeview, Paisley, and Crane). The high school at Crane is unique in being the only publicly-supported boarding school in the United States. Some students must travel more than 100 miles to attend. There are no colleges in the area, although various college courses are offered during summer sessions at the Malheur Field Station, south of Burns.

Beef cattle, wood products, tourism, and government activities are major industries in the region. Vast acreages of public rangeland and forest provide summer forage for the cattle industry, and public forest lands are the principal sources of commercial timber. Most private land is classified as rangeland or forest, with relatively small acreages in certain valleys being suitable for crops and pastures.

Although some soils are rich, a short growing season and limited water supplies restrict agricultural diversity. Flood irrigation, using water from snowpacks in mountain ranges, is used on native meadows, which produce hay for winter cattle feed. Recently, using heavy equipment, improved well-digging equipment, and modern sprinkling systems, farmers have been able to clear large tracts of sagebrush and greasewood to grow alfalfa and grain. Although other crops are being tried on an experimental basis, none currently generates a significant income for the area's farmers. The high salt content of soils and water from some wells makes long-term irrigation somewhat risky.

In 1976, income from Harney County farms and ranches was about $11 million. Anyone accustomed to hearing Harney County ranchers complain about weather and prices may be surprised to learn that only Clackamas, among Oregon's 36 counties, has a higher percentage of households with income exceeding $15,000 per year. Lake County has a higher percentage of families below the poverty level than does Harney County.

Lumber mills in Hines (with logging operations near Seneca) and Lakeview are major employers in the two counties. The Hines Mill has about 1,100 employees. Lumber and plywood are the major wood products. Ponderosa pine is the principal species harvested, with Douglas fir, larch, and true firs making up the remainder.

From a recent document prepared in Harney County, one gets an idea of the area's desperation in attempting to attract manufacturing industry. After citing the area's virtues (e.g., wide-open spaces, an abundance of female labor, lack of congestion, etc.), the document suggests that some enterprising industry might wish to blend sagebrush and juniper leaves into wax candles to produce marketable, pleasant odors characteristic of the West.

In the Great Basin region of Oregon, tourism and recreation, which tend to be more important farther north and west, probably account for less than 15% of total retail sales. Although the region offers many delights to the visitor, it is largely undiscovered and attracts relatively few, who come only to see the sights. The current trend favors a decrease in the number of people who visit the area to harvest its resources (hunting, fishing, artifact hunting, etc.) and an increase in the number who come to share the natural wonders and historical richness. More people are discovering the remote places, and large groups come to study the area's geology, vegetation, animals, and natural history. Through traffic on major highways contributes significantly to the local economy, especially in Burns and Lakeview.

Hunting has always been a major attraction in the area. Mule deer, pronghorns, elk (mainly in the southern Blue Mountains), bighorn sheep, cottontails, waterfowl, mourning doves, ring-necked pheasants, and several species of upland game birds are hunted. In the early 1970's, when mule deer were exceedingly abundant, opening day hunters doubled or tripled populations of some counties. Recently reduced herds and four-point buck or better requirements have drastically reduced the number of hunters. Chukars, the most popular upland game bird, attract many hunters to remote canyons and mountains. Waterfowl hunting, once a major attraction in the area, has declined to minor importance.

91

Several lakes, especially Fish Lake and Mann Lake, numerous reservoirs, and many mountain streams provide fishing in the area. Most streams are small, cannot withstand heavy fishing pressure, and must be protected with special restrictions. Popular sites, such as Fish Lake and the Blitzen River near Frenchglen, must be planted with hatchery trout to sustain fishing demands.

In recent years the basin has attracted increasingly large numbers of rock hounds. Obsidian, thundereggs, agates, opal, petrified wood, jasper, and sunstones are to be found. In some areas, collectors have removed most of the available supply, e.g., a petrified wood site near Narrows.

In the past, many people have come to the area to collect Indian artifacts. This practice, encouraged by chamber-of-commerce leaflets, should be discouraged (see Chapter 9). The supply of artifacts has dwindled sufficiently to discourage all but the most avid pothunters. Most abandoned town sites in the area, although still interesting to visit, have long since been picked clean of bottles and other items attractive to collectors.

Although many campers visit the area, there are few officially designated campgrounds, but most of those available are in beautiful surroundings and provide great enjoyment to users. The Bureau of Land Management operates campgrounds at Page Springs, Fish Lake, Jackman Park, and Blitzen Crossing on Steens Mountain. Camping is also permitted in restricted areas of Hart Mountain National Antelope Refuge. Other campgrounds are provided by the U.S. Forest Service in forests of the northern parts of the basin region. Camping is permitted only at Krumbo Reservoir on the Malheur National Wildlife Refuge, and most visitors arrange to stay at the Malheur Field Station. Many attractive and interesting areas in the basin, although vast, have no designated camping sites or facilities (e.g., the Alvord Basin and surrounding drainages, the Catlow Valley, the Warner Valley, etc.).

The largest number of visitors to the area come to see the land and its wildlife. About 15,000 people visit Malheur Refuge each year—primarily to see the large numbers of birds, especially waterfowl and wading birds. Steens Mountain is awe-inspiring and attracts many who wish only to enjoy the magnificent view from the top. Others come to see bighorns, though few do, and pronghorns. Many are thrilled to see their first coyotes, eagles, or deer. In the future, the wildlife, vistas, hot springs, playas, geology, glacial gorges, and other attractions should become increasingly important resources and produce a tourist trade vastly exceeding that of the past, which was based on use of the resources rather than enjoying, seeing, photographing, and leaving it in place.

Gravel, sand, and volcanic ash are about the only commercially valuable materials mined in the area. Deposits of zeolite and diatomite, industrial materials, occur, but have attracted little commercial interest. The northwestern portion of Oregon's Great Basin region offers attractive potential for oil and gas exploration, and drilling leases on public lands are increasing. Uranium has been mined near Lakeview, mercury in the Steens, and minor amounts of gold in northern Harney County. Although other deposits of metallic minerals are known, e.g., antimony, copper, lead, zinc, and molybdenum, these cannot be mined profitably at the present time. When higher grade deposits are exhausted elsewhere, some of these may become commercially valuable.

For about 10 years preceding 1902, a borax industry operated in the Alvord Basin. Hot springs in and near Borax Lake contain about 80 parts per million borate. Spring water flows out onto the surrounding desert, evaporates, and leaves a thick white crust of sodium borate (5 to 20% boric acid content) and numerous other sodium salts. The Rose Valley Borax Company hired Chinese workers to collect the salt crust into small piles during the summer. A new crust formed very quickly. The salts were dissolved in two large vats (6,000 to 8,000 gallons) by boiling them with water and acid. The brine was transferred to 24 crystallizing tanks (1,200 gallons each). Sagebrush was used to fire the dissolving tanks. When the solution cooled, crystallized borax was collected, sacked, and shipped by 16-mule team to the Central Pacific Railroad in Winnemucca (130 miles). About 400 tons of refined borax were shipped each year. Today the remnants of the two large dissolving vats still remain at the site, and a sod house, which housed the Chinese laborers, still stands. Borax, used primarily as a cleaning compound, has attracted new interests as additional uses have been discovered (e.g., fuel additive, fire retardant, etc.), but there have been no further attempts to exploit the Alvord deposits.

Currently, there are no commercial plants generating electricity within the area. Hydroelectric power is imported and sold by private companies or cooperatives. Portions of the northern Great Basin have been designated as Known Geothermal Resource Areas, and the BLM has leased large tracts near Lakeview, in the Warner Valley, in the Alvord Basin, near Harney Lake, and elsewhere, for exploration of geothermal potential. Most leases are held by major oil companies. No commercial developments of geothermal resources are currently active in the region.

Because the number of sunny days generally exceeds 300, there are good prospects for use of solar power. In many places in the basin, the use of wind to generate electricity offers good potential. Windmills, once commonly used to pump water, have been largely replaced by electric pumps.

In summary, Oregon's Great Basin region still retains much of the flavor of the old West—community dances, cattle drives, and strong ties with former times. Whiskey is still drunk straight from the bottle, and bars are better attended than churches. A small minority of wealthy landowners tends to exert strong influences on public opinion and community affairs. Probably because so much land is available, local land ethics are not the most desirable. In many ways the people are an enigma—the majority register as Democrats, but community thinking tends to be conservative or even ultra-conservative with respect to liberal ideas, minorities, fashions, and any social or behavioral deviations from accepted standards. A desire for new growth and industry conflicts with a yearning for the past. Although individualism is proclaimed and federal agencies are generally disdained, the entire welfare of the area is totally dependent upon publicly-owned rangelands and forest. The long domination of private interest at the expense of public interests lags far behind changes made elsewhere in the state. Yet, the region has a great deal to offer the visitor, and there are many cowboys just waiting in numerous small, remote hamlets to advise tourists who seek direction that, "There is no way to get there from here."

CHAPTER 9

Environmental Problems

Every region has environmental problems, but the Great Basin has some unique ones. Because rainfall is scant, the soils are fragile, ecosystems are in precarious balance, and land is incapable of tolerating sustained disturbance. Unfortunately, despite the fragility of arid land and desert, these areas are often thought of as worthless wastelands and treated contemptuously. Like islands at sea, basins of internal drainage have been isolated and protected for long periods, during which they developed well-adjusted ecosystems. These areas have never been exposed to forces similar to man or his domestic animals, and the climate and the resources lack the resiliency for coping with technology, wanton greed, and unmindful acts. Damage may take generations to heal. In his resource management, carelessness, and ignorance, but mainly in quest of the dollar, man has injured and defaced much of the land.

We are told that the pioneers came west convinced that there were no limits to the land and resources. In the Great Basin, settlers claimed the best bottom land for themselves, but enjoyed unrestricted use of the public domain. Often, by controlling available water supplies, a landowner could assure himself of the use of surrounding public lands. There were no fences, even on home properties, until about 1885. As early as 1880, Central Oregon ranges were overstocked with cattle, and much of the area was overgrazed. In the last half of the 19th century, sheep raising flourished, and by the 1890's sheep outnumbered cattle. Unlike cattlemen, who usually had base properties, many sheepmen were nomads without a home base; flocks were taken to higher elevations in the summertime and down to the desert in the winter. Forests and public ranges were used without cost. Cattlemen resented the intrusion of sheep, and in Crook County, they formed a sheep shooter's association and even reported annual kills to newpapers. By 1901 there were at least 140,000 sheep on Steens Mountain, and more than 100,000 continued to graze there in the 1920's. At the same time immense herds of privately-owned and feral horses roamed freely over the range.

By the turn of the century, ranges were in a pitiful state. In 1906 the U.S. Forest Service was established and began issuing grazing allotments, charging a small grazing fee, and attempting to reduce grazing abuses. But during World War I, when the nation needed meat, leather, and wool, restrictions were patriotically set aside. By the end of the war, grazing lands on national forests had been ravaged. Meanwhile, public domain lands were unprotected and exploited as stockmen saw fit.

The total effects of overgrazing will never be fully known, because it all happened before the original vegetation could be studied—before the science of range management even existed. But we know some of the consequences. Soils were laid bare to wind and water erosion, and the protective crust of soil organisms (e.g., lichens, mosses, etc.) was destroyed. Watersheds were damaged. Stream banks were eroded, causing streams to be wider, shallower, and full of silt. Destruction of stream-side cover, increasing water temperatures and decreasing invertebrate life, affected fish populations.

The species composition of vegetation was drastically altered by overgrazing. Native bunchgrasses, although deep rooted and drought resistant, were unable to tolerate overgrazing and early spring trampling. These perennial grasses were replaced by sagebrush, rabbitbrush, and other shrubs. Today some areas support 6,000 to 7,000 sagebrush plants per acre—up to 80% of the vegetative stand. On severely overgrazed lands, individual sagebrush plants are separated by bare soil, and fire, a useful range tool, will not carry from plant to plant, except with strong winds. But when the wind is strong, there is danger of uncontrollable range fires. Overgrazing encourages spread of cheatgrass, Russian thistle, halogeton, and other undesirable weeds. Although cheat is an indicator of overgrazing, stockmen like it, because it is often the only early spring forage available.

An overgrazed range recovers very slowly, in fact no one knows how much time is required. Some 10-acre plots at the Squaw Butte Experiment Station (west of Burns) have not been grazed for 40 years, but they look no different than the surrounding land, which has been grazed every year.

In 1934 Congress passed the Taylor Grazing Act, which divided public domain lands into grazing districts, established a grazing allotment system, assessed minimal grazing fees, and required holders of grazing allotments to own a base property. The Grazing Service was formed to administer the act. In 1946, the Grazing Service and Land Office, which had been responsible for getting rid of public domain, through land grants, and keeping records of its progress, were combined to form the Bureau of Land Management. It should be noted that the BLM inherited lands that

In Oregon's Great Basin country, sunsets often generate spectacular displays of color.

The Alvord Desert blanketed with snow. Winter in the high desert can be harsh but scenic.

*Fort Rock—a major geological landmark
and source of valuable primitive artifacts.*

*Former shorelines of pluvial lakes are
visible in interior basins, such as Warner Valley.*

Faulting is common in the Great Basin;
this fault is in a roadcut 13 miles west of Denio.

Prevailing winds build dune systems
on the lee side of playas such as Harney Lake.

*Desert pavement in the
Alvord Basin near Borax Lake.*

*The Alvord Desert, a large playa,
contrasted against the Steens Mountain scarp.*

*Big Indian—one of several
spectacular glaciated gorges on Steens Mountain.*

*The large seeds of piñon pine
were a staple food for Basin Indians.*

Pictographs (shown here) and petroglyphs are commonly found in the Great Basin.

Sign in Catlow Valley points to non-existent towns once inhabited by homesteaders.

*Crustose lichens brighten
many high desert cliffs and boulders.*

*In the fall, aspen transforms Hart Mountain
and other desert ranges into a blaze of color.*

*Zones of plants encroaching on Lily Lake
on Steens Mountain illustrate hydrarch succession.*

*Shooting stars—one of the many
decorative flowering plants of the high country.*

Butterflies visiting orange sneezeweed, a conspicuous summertime plant on Steens Mountain.

One of several species of Indian-paintbrush found in the northern Great Basin.

A veritable eruption of sagebrush bells on a mudflat in the Warner Valley.

Ephedra (Mormon tea), a medicinal plant of the Great Basin, extends north to near Fields.

*Iodine bush, a salt-tolerant species grows
in the Alvord Basin and at Badwater in Death Valley.*

*The call and silhouette of California
Quail are familiar to most desert visitors.*

*Greater sandhill cranes—a major attraction
at Malheur Refuge (photo by C.D. Littlefield).*

*Cliff swallow nests. Today many
nests are built on man-made structures.*

Desert horned lizard—a
common species in the Alvord Basin.

Spadefoot toads are one of the
few amphibians well-adapted to desert habitats.

*A paucity of trees in the desert forces
birds, such as nighthawks, to roost in strange places.*

*The cow is the most conspicuous animal
in the West and dominates the economy and ecology.*

*Hot springs and glory pools are
scattered throughout Oregon's Great Basin country.*

*Geothermal exploration on the Alvord Desert
illustrates the conflict between uses of resources.*

*Mining claim in the
mineral-rich Pueblo Mountains.*

*Steens Mountain, Oregon's largest
fault block, represents many things to many people.*

had been up for grabs for nearly 75 years—lands that no one wanted.

The Taylor Act brought an end to unrestricted use of public lands by nomadic sheepmen and horse raisers, who simply let horses run free. But stockmen were accustomed to free access to public ranges and were vigorously opposed to any governmental restrictions (and they still are). The use of these lands was considered a right—not a privilege. Although the disgraceful conditions of public land had forced Congress to act, pressures from the livestock industry were monumental, and the Taylor Act became a compromise. Likewise, the BLM was formed by combining two defunct and toothless agencies and shackled by advisory committees of ranchers, unsympathetic western congressmen and senators, and miserly budgets. The BLM was not intended to have any real clout, and to make certain, their boss, the Secretary of Interior, is always a westerner—supposedly one who understands the stockmen's needs.

But times do change. Increased public interest in the out-of-doors and the age of environmental concern are beginning to tell Congress and the livestock industry that public lands belong to the public. The BLM hired competent people, began to manage the land, and to everyone's surprise, began growing some teeth. Cattle are no longer permitted on the range too early in the spring—which was the cause of much range devastation. The results of range surveys are used to decide permissible grazing pressures, and many other good range practices are used. But the BLM is still largely dominated by the livestock industry and subjected to strong local and political pressures. The agency's claims of multiple use merely mean that one must share a campground with cattle. Wildlife, watersheds, and other non-forage resources continue to be secondary to livestock. But the Bureau of Land Management has made tremendous progress, and the 1976 Federal Land Policy Act (Organic Act), while imperfect, should provide further strength.

The livestock industry, like many special interest groups, has great political influence and knows how to use it. In the 1940's the industry and a few western politicians even tried to steal the public resource lands. This incredible and flagrant episode is told in detail by Voigt (see Selected Readings and References). The BLM, Forest Service, and even federal wildlife refuges know well the political power of the industry. Grazing is permitted on Malheur National Wildlife Refuge and Hart Mountain National Antelope Refuge. A visitor to Malheur Refuge may wonder why more than 200 miles of internal fences are needed to raise ducks!

Stockmen have successfully avoided paying a fair price for public forage and have stubbornly resisted all attempts to reduce grazing on public lands. Congress has failed to support the BLM or Forest Service in efforts to reduce grazing, even when disastrous range conditions dictated such a course. Today when the range is degraded, range improvements are substituted for grazing reductions. Crested wheatgrass seedings are an example of such range improvements and are done at public expense.

Improved management of public ranges requires broad public insistence upon real multiple use and active citizen support of the federal agencies responsible for managing public lands in the public's interest.

Horses had relatively humble beginnings as small, multiple-toed creatures of the forest, but 60 million years later, they emerged as large, fleet-footed animals of the plains. Much of the evolutionary history of horses is recorded in fossil beds in Oregon and elsewhere in the West. But even though horses evolved in North America, they disappeared from the New World about 8,000 years ago, and did not return until introduced by Spanish conquistadors—probably around the year 1520. Spanish horses apparently reached Oregon in about 1750. In 1804, the Lewis and Clark expedition found that Indians in Idaho and eastern Oregon owned herds of horses, some of which still carried Spanish brands. But the Nez Perce had already developed their own breed of horse—the Appaloosa.

When Indians were confined to reservations and white men began to raise horses on the open range, many horses escaped and ran wild. Because range horses are derived from escaped stock, they are more properly termed "feral" than "wild"; there is little Spanish horse ancestry left in them.

In the 19th century an estimated 2 million feral horses roamed western rangelands. Many were gathered for use in World War I or sold to other warring nations. Thousands were caught and used as dog food or in other products. Because of the damage feral horses do to the range, they are despised by stockmen. Unlike cattle and sheep, horses have upper incisors and are able to graze closer to the soil and pull up plants by the roots. They are primarily grazers and directly compete with domestic stock for forage. Because horses are on the range all year, they do much damage from trampling—particularly in the early spring. In the winter they paw away snow or move to south-facing slopes, and unless the range is badly depleted, do not often winter kill, although some die, usually in February and March. Herds may increase at a rate of 20% per year.

Feral horses prefer high ground and run in small herds consisting of a stallion and his harem of mares and younger animals. When young males are about 3 years old, they are driven away and form bachelor herds, but when they reach 6 or 7 years of age, they begin to challenge stallions in charge of established harems. Fighting can be extremely vicious. Although feral horses come in all colors, sizes, and shapes, they tend to be smaller than domestic breeds and are often runty and poorly formed.

As feral horses declined in number, they became a matter of intense and emotional controversy. Largely under the leadership of Velma Johnson, a Reno secretary—better known as "Wild Horse Annie"—organized groups began to defend the rights of feral horses on public lands. Such groups point to the role of the horse in taming the West, consider horses part of the American heritage, and contend that horses have as much right on public lands as do domestic cattle and sheep. Ranchers and others, concerned with range damage, argue that feral horses, like house sparrows, starlings, weeds, and other introductions, have no original claim to the land. Federal land managers are apt to view the horses as an asset, while seeking to keep their numbers manageable.

The movie "The Misfits" (Clark Gable and Marilyn Monroe) and public revulsion against wholesale slaughter of feral horses resulted in legislative action designed to provide protection. In 1959, legislation dubbed the Wild Horse Annie Act, prohibited the pursuit and capture of feral horses with mechanized vehicles. By 1969, feral horses numbered only 16,000 and in 1971, the Wild Horse and Burro Act placed range horses and burros under the care of the BLM. Private citizens were not permitted to harass horses, and stockmen were given 90 days to claim any privately owned horse on public resource lands.

During the 1970's herds increased to 14,000 burros (a serious problem in Death Valley) and 60,000 horses in the 11 Western states (60-70% of which are in Nevada). In Oregon there are about 7,000 horses (only a few burros), and 50% of them reside in the Burns BLM district. In 1976, the Steens Mountain herd was estimated at 1,200 head. During this period of rapid increase of horse herds, the BLM could not legally capture range horses with the aid of mechanized vehicles and had to chase them on horseback, using decoy herds of domestic horses and strategically located corrals to capture them. The cost per horse captured averaged about $500 and ran as high as $800 in difficult and rough terrain. Injury to men and saddle horses was considerable. The estimated cost per capture with a helicopter is about $50. Captured horses are given to private citizens who request them, but under current law, the BLM retains actual ownership of the animals.

The Federal Land Policy and Management Act of 1976 authorized the BLM to use helicopters in horse and burro management. Hopefully, this will bring the long dispute about range horses to a happy ending and final solution—feral horses, but in manageable numbers.

Unfortunately too many of us gained our first impressions of predators from "Little Red Riding Hood" and similar childhood tales. What is even more unfortunate is that some people, as they become adults and sometimes public office holders, retain infantile notions of predators. No aspect of American life is more muddled and incongruent than our attitudes about predators and predator management. We have paid bounties on coyotes, and then had to pay bounties on jackrabbits. The controversy over predator control continues, but somewhat abated by a series of recent factors.

Mutton and wool have fallen into disfavor. After the Taylor Grazing Act, the huge bands of sheep disappeared from public rangelands, and in Oregon sheep were raised in smaller bands on farms and ranches. In the northern Great Basin, sheep practically disappeared, and with them, much of the controversy over predators. Coyotes do kill sheep (the 1970 loss in 12 western states was estimated at $22,300,000), but the number of sheep lost was small compared to the number grazed.

In Oregon the bear and cougar, both relatively rare, are now designated as game animals and managed as a resource by the Oregon State Department of Fish and Game. Wolverines and kit foxes, because of their endangered status, are fully protected by law. Only the coyote and red fox continue to be designated as predators and managed by the state Department of Agriculture. In a state proclaiming enlightened resource management, this illogical and vestigial arrangement is an outright concession to the livestock industry. High pelt prices and wanton destruction pushed the bobcat close to extinction in Oregon, before the 1977 legislature transferred the bobcat from predator to game status. The red fox if of no great interest east of the Cascades.

Coyotes have been shot, trapped, poisoned with strychnine, and their pups dug from dens and killed. In the early 1940's, the "coyote getter" came into widespread use. The original version was a cartridge-powered cyanide gun, which was later replaced by a spring-powered device (the M-44). The M-44 is a pipe driven in the ground and baited with a tuft of scented wool. When the trigger is pulled, a charge of cyanide is fired into the animal's mouth. The M-44 kills coyotes and dogs (or whatever happens to trigger it), but does not harm large numbers of other animals, as do poison baits.

In the late 1940's thallium sulfate and 1080 (sodium monoflouroacetate) came into popular use at poison bait stations. Both of these poisons killed large numbers of non-target animals, including eagles, kit foxes, and others, and the federal predator control agency ceased using thallium because of its extreme toxicity. Then in 1971 a special advisory committee on predator control studied existing predator control problems and made numerous observations and recommendations in a widely publicized report, the Cain Report, named for the chairman, Stanley A. Cain (see Selected Readings and References).

The Cain Report noted that of the control methods used at that time, only shooting and killing pups at dens were selective against coyotes. Also, the report pointed out that although 1080 caused wholesale losses among non-target animals, its use had not substantially reduced livestock losses. In response to the Cain Report and to public indignation caused by a series of eagle poisonings, President Nixon issued an executive order prohibiting use of all poisons, except in emergencies, on public lands. Also, federal personnel were ordered to cease using poisons on private lands.

In response to pressures brought by the states, livestock industry, and others, the Environmental Protection Agency has again authorized use of the M-44 by official predator control agents—not private individuals. Because the device is reasonably specific, environmental groups favored its use, rather than traps, which are inhumane and dangerous to many kinds of animals.

The Cain Report and recent research findings have produced other needed changes. The Division of Wildlife Services, the federal agency responsible for predator control, has become much better informed, more professional, and less responsive to unwarranted demands for predator control. Because haphazard reductions of coyote numbers merely stimulate higher reproductive rates, control measures are now aimed at individual guilty coyotes, rather than broad-scale prophylactic control. Also, Oregon, which in some years has spent more on predator control than the value of its livestock losses, has developed programs of public education and hired extension personnel to work with predator problems.

Much of what is known about coyote diets has come from studies of stomach contents. Where the hair of deer or cattle are found, there is no way of knowing whether the hair is from carrion or from a victim of predation. Coyotes do kill fawns, and the total impact upon deer herds depends upon the abundance of alternative foods (e.g., rabbits), weather, and other variables. Deer losses are not normally a cause for concern. Although sheep losses can be serious, losses of cattle seem to be greatly exaggerated, especially if one considers the benefits of coyotes in rodent and rabbit control. In any event, if private livestock are to be grazed on public lands, predator control must be done in ways that are acceptable to the general public.

A special case involves predator problems on wildlife refuges, where, at considerable expense, ideal conditions have been created to attract large numbers of wildlife. In these circumstances, predators enjoy easy pickings, much the same as the fox inside the hen house. At Malheur Refuge, ravens, which nest on nearby rims and on abandoned windmill platforms in Malheur Lake, destroy large numbers of crane and waterfowl eggs. In some years raccoons are quite destructive. Coyotes cause little damage, except in years after jackrabbit populations have crashed. Because the refuge is not essential habitat to these predators, but represents the last remnants of formerly extensive waterfowl breeding areas, some judicious predator control seems warranted.

Huge numbers of blackbirds nest on Malheur Refuge. As large acreages of nearby desert are plowed and planted to grains, it is only a matter of time until grain farmers begin to complain about blackbird depredation of crops. The problem has already reached serious proportions near Princeton.

Water is a precious resource in desert regions, and its ownership, uses, quality, and distribution are of vital concern. For example, Malheur Lake, one of the nation's largest freshwater marshes and the most prominent asset at Malheur National Wildlife Refuge, receives part of its water supply from the Silvies River. Although the Silvies is a fairly large stream, draining about 1,200 square miles, much of the flow is diverted for irrigation and fails to reach the lake. Even in 1972, a wet year when 28% of Malheur Lake's flow came from the Silvies, no water reached the lake after about July 10, and about two-thirds of the flow did not get that far. In 1973, only 1% of the inflow came from the Silvies, and flow ceased during the first week of April. Upstream from the lake, 122,700 acres of cropland are irrigated from streamflow sources in the Silvies River Basin.

As long ago as 1903-1904 there was discussion about damming the Silvies, and in the 1950's, the U.S. Corps of Engineers became seriously interested. The Corps continued studying the feasibility of providing upstream storage for flood control, irrigation, and recreation—all the usual benefits. Although some people favored a dam, most were unwilling to risk changing from flood irrigation to a more conventional system. Those holding water rights and getting full benefit of spring floods were unwilling to settle for less. But the major obstacle was fear that such a dam might upset the delicate and precarious ecological balance of Malheur Lake. Because of possible damage to the lake and the absence of a clear mandate from local people, the Corps has abandoned plans for the dam—at least for the moment.

Large numbers of irrigation wells are being drilled in the Harney, Catlow, and Alvord-Pueblo basins. The specific effects of large-scale use of these underground water sources are as yet unknown. Neither water-yielding capacity nor safe use limits have been determined. Many wells in these areas contain excessive amounts of salts, especially boron and sodium, and some deliver water that is unfit for drinking or use on crops. Of 59 wells tested, 39 were judged to be satisfactory, 10 marginal, and 10 unsatisfactory.

Poor distribution of water holes on ranges causes vexing problems. During hot weather, cattle spend the day near water and move out to feed at night and during the cool hours. This behavior causes excessive trampling and overgrazing near water, creating sacrifice areas, but results in undergrazing of forage located farther from water. Under some conditions, cattle can get by with drinking every other day and will trail a mile to water. As ranchers and federal agencies create new sources of surface water in an attempt to get better use of the range, they may inadvertently benefit wildlife. Some areas that were formerly waterless now have larger game populations (e.g., pronghorns and sage grouse) near man-made water holes. Some artificial watering sites are large enough to be stocked with fish and may attract a few nesting waterfowl. Water holes and wildlife on grazing lands tend to encourage multiple uses.

Any time foreign animals are introduced into an area, there is a possibility that native animals will suffer as a consequence. The potential danger is accentuated in areas of internal drainage, where species may have existed for long periods without stressful competition. A vigorous introduced species may either replace a native species, or, in the absence of natural controls and predators, become an abundant pest.

Carp were first brought to the United States from France in 1831 and 1832. In 1877, the U.S. Fish Commission obtained stocks from Germany, and in 1879, federal hatcheries distributed fingerling carp to 38 states and territories. By 1897, carp had become a recognized pest in many places, and fishery biologists realized that the haphazard introductions had been a serious mistake.

In the early 1920's, carp were introduced into the Silvies River (they may have been brought in as early as 1882). By 1955 waters at Malheur Refuge were teeming with carp, and 1.5 million (20-25 inches long) were rotenoned. Although the carp were partially removed on other occasions (as recently as 1977), populations rapidly returned and currently inhabit nearly all Harney Basin waters. By riling bottom muds and sediments, carp are believed to reduce penetration of sunlight and discourage growth of many submerged aquatic plants (e.g., sago pondweed)—thus, drastically reducing food supplies for migratory waterfowl in Malheur Lake.

Numerous other species of fish have been introduced into the northern Great Basin from eastern North America (e.g., various sunfish, catfish, perch, etc.). The consequences, if any, of these introductions upon native fish or other animals are unknown.

Bullfrogs have been introduced in the Harney Basin and have spread widely. Because bullfrogs are large, voracious feeders, they are able to prey upon a great many smaller animals. The native spotted frog and perhaps other animals may be unable to compete. Bullfrogs are known to have exterminated indigenous species of frogs in other localities in the West.

Among birds, introduced house sparrows and starlings compete with many native birds for nesting sites, food, and other essentials. Both of these species are aggressive and will drive much larger birds from a feeder.

In treeless portions of the high desert, many types of birds perch on, and hunt from, utility poles. Hawks, owls, eagles, and ravens are often electrocuted when they touch the wires on transformer poles. In some areas protective sheaths are placed around transformers to prevent such accidents, and in places where there are few natural perches, this practice should be encouraged.

Fences also serve as perches, but can be death traps as well. Most cattle fences are four or five strands of barbed wire and too tall to be easily negotiated by small deer. A fawn or even an adult may partially clear the top wire, but get their hind legs tangled in the wires. Such animals suffer severely as they await slow death from starvation, thirst, and exhaustion. On Malheur Refuge, some fences have been converted to four strands, with the top strand lowered and bottom strand raised. A couple hundred miles of internal fences on the refuge serve as obstacles to flying birds accustomed to wide-open spaces and uncluttered terrain. Grebes and ducks have been found impaled and hanging from barbed wire fences. At least one trumpeter swan died after colliding with a barbed wire fence. Because the extensive fence system serves only cattle, it should be removed from a wildlife refuge inhabited by thousands of waterfowl and wading birds. The posts could be left for perches.

Unlike most states, Oregon has a rich potential for producing geothermal energy. However, if all geothermal sites in the state were developed, only about 5% of the state's energy needs would be met. Because many geothermal sites are unique, beautiful, and wild, there is much to be lost from such developments. But with the national energy shortage, Congress has instructed the BLM to explore and develop these energy resources.

Most of the geothermal sites in southeastern Oregon are far from centers of population, thus any electricity produced is likely to be transported over ugly transmission lines to California or other densely populated areas. Geothermal development in unique places such as the Alvord Desert would disfigure a beautiful landscape, disrupt desert ecosystems, hasten residential sprawl in remote areas, increase sanitation problems, and cause a host of other environmental concerns. One has to ask if all these problems would justify the seemingly small advantages—especially if one considers future generations, who have yet to admire the beauty of the Alvord Desert.

The menace of off-road vehicles, while creating extensive devastation in California deserts and in the southern Great Basin, is only now becoming a serious problem in Oregon's Great Basin region. In deserts, off-road vehicles encourage wind and water erosion, leave unsightly tracks, compact soil (often destroying plant root systems), destroy shrubs, encourage weeds, interrupt food chains, and cause other damage that can take decades or centuries to mend. Tracks made by jeeps and tanks during military training maneuvers in the Mohave Desert in the 1940's are still not healed.

Driving motorcycles, dune buggies, and 4-wheel drive vehicles has become a major recreation. Although organized races and established desert trails cause great damage, persons wandering aimlessly from established roads constitute a greater threat. Unfortunately, those who drive off-road vehicles are like everyone else—they are drawn to the most interesting places—areas having abundant wildlife, interesting vegetation, archeological sites, and other attractions. Although off-road vehicles are a socially acceptable form of recreation among part of the population, surveys show that most people visit deserts to see and do things that are jeopardized by the vehicles. The defunct notion that semi-arid and desert areas are worthless seems to be part of the justification. Because much of the destruction is caused by individuals, rather than organized special interest groups, the problem of off-road vehicles is difficult to combat. Professional activities, such as the celebrated attempts upon world land speed records on the Alvord

Desert in 1976, are much easier to regulate and supervise.

On Forest Service lands, too many roads have caused problems in the management of big game. Forest Service sales policies require logging contractors to build good forest roads during their logging operations. These roads have given poachers easy access to millions of acres of remote and difficult-to-patrol land. Even "legal" hunters can form task forces along systems of road grids and use citizen band radios to report the position and direction of travel of deer or elk. Under these conditions, game animals have little chance to escape. The state of Oregon has closed particularly vulnerable areas to all hunting. These logging roads, while useful for fire prevention and forest management, have endangered another resource and represent a good example of bad planning.

Artifact hunters, with the encouragement and blessings of local tourist agencies, have done much of their collecting on public lands in violation of various acts designed to protect national antiquities. Amateurs and curio hunters have ruined many valuable archeological sites, by screening large quantities of soil, excavating shelters, and removing everything of interest. Although some professional archeological work has been done in the region, a large amount of useful material has already been removed by "pothunters". Several pictographs and petroglyphs have been defaced with spray paint or gouged by vandals.

Although rock and fossil hunting is generally harmless, some areas have been severely damaged by commercial collectors and over-enthusiastic individuals who have used backhoes and even dynamite to remove large petrified logs. Pits large enough to hold an automobile are left to scar the landscape.

Many of the area's remaining ghost towns are being vandalized and abused by collectors. Bottles and other valuable items have long since been stolen. Signs, weathered lumber (for antique picture frames), and other objects are now disappearing. At Blitzen, beer cans and other garbage have been left among the old buildings, and at least one party camped on the site and built a bon-fire of lumber torn from buildings. Why would anyone want to visit a ghost town and then tear it apart and burn it?

The most recent threat to desert areas is increased residential sprawl. Better well-digging equipment and the availability of large mobile homes have made it possible for many to establish homes on almost any site—no matter how remote. And electric utilities obligingly run utility lines right to the door. People have claimed marginal land before. In 1914 about 700 people homesteaded the Catlow Valley, and in 1934, under the battle cry of "Birds or Babies, Which?", settlers and promoters stormed into the dry bed of Malheur Lake and farmed it. But today, people take all of life's comforts with them when they settle on marginal land. These people are not likely to be driven out by adversity or the elements. If serious problems are to be averted and the landscape protected, responsible authorities must pass suitable zoning ordinances and strictly enforce them. Currently, residential sprawl is encouraged.

People have always chased around deserts looking for pots of gold. Such people have missed seeing the only real gold the desert offers—an occasional rainbow, hundreds of fantastic sunsets, interesting and secretive animals, pungent aromas of desert shrubs, droplets of dew on a hairy leaf, and a thousand other delights. As with every generation, we are duty bound to preserve all these for desert lovers yet to be born.

CHAPTER 10

Natural History Attractions

The Great Basin is full of natural wonders, beauty, and charm. A visitor to the desert can find reward and delight by watching the antics of insects on a shrub, or by observing Nature's design and wisdom in a small patch of desert, or by witnessing an incredible sun descend beyond a horizon that defies description. Desert vistas can rejuvenate the spirit and lead the visitor toward a lifetime of pleasure. Although curiosity and personal satisfaction can be rewarding guides, Oregon's Great Basin country offers some special attractions that should not be missed. This chapter describes some of these special places where a sojourn and close inspection might be worthwhile. In Chapter 11, many of the same sites are included in recommended auto tours.

Malheur National Wildlife Refuge—After glacial times, the Harney Basin contained remnants of a large pluvial lake, extensive marshes, meadows, and other aquatic environments. The basin was a major stopping place for countless flocks of migratory birds and supported tremendous nesting populations of waterfowl, wading birds, shorebirds, and avian life of most every description. Fur bearers, big game, and other wildlife further enriched a fantastic natural wealth that had attracted and helped sustain generations of primitive people. Captain Charles E. Bendire, who was stationed at Camp Harney from 1875 to 1877, first studied and attempted to catalogue the teeming bird life of the Harney Basin. Later, the popular press carried accounts of the unbelievable bird wealth of the area.

An increasing population of settlers enjoyed unrestricted harvest of the birds for food and other uses. Then plume hunters, seeking the frills of a demanding millinery industry, came to harvest this great resource. The results were devastating— especially to the colonies of nesting birds at Malheur Lake. The great egret population was exterminated, and other species were diminished or threatened. On 18 August 1908, in response to the press and public outrage, President Theodore Roosevelt issued a special executive order (later changed to a proclamation) creating the Lake Malheur Reservation. The order set aside Malheur, Mud, and Harney lakes as a sanctuary for breeding birds. The U.S. Department of Agriculture was responsible for administering the reservation.

In 1934 Malheur Lake became dry because of continuing drought and diversion of upstream water supplies for irrigation. In order to gain control of water sources essential to Malheur Lake, the federal government purchased 64,000 acres in the Blitzen Valley in 1935. The land, obtained from the Eastern Oregon Livestock Company for $675,000, had once belonged to Peter French and included the famous P Ranch. The expanded refuge was administered by the Bureau of Biological Survey (USDA), and Stanley Jewett was named manager. In 1939, the bureau was transferred to the Department of the Interior, and in 1940, the U.S. Fish and Wildlife Service was created and made responsible for refuges. John Scharff, perhaps the best known manager of Malheur Refuge, took over in 1939 and held the position until 1971. When about 6,000 acres were purchased in the Warm Springs Valley near the Double O Ranch in 1940, the refuge, except for minor changes, attained its present size and shape.

Today the refuge, still administered by the U.S. Fish and Wildlife Service, is one of the Nation's largest and includes the largest freshwater marsh in the United States. The refuge contains about 181,000 acres and is shaped like a lopsided "T", extending from Frenchglen to the north shore of Malheur Lake (41 miles) and from the east shore of Malheur Lake to a few miles west of the Double O Station (37 miles). Although the original wildlife grandeur is much diminished, because of declining continental populations and local management problems (e.g., overgrazing of cattle), Malheur Refuge remains a major attraction to bird watchers, wildlife photographers, and other visitors.

From 1935 to 1941, three camps of the Civilian Conservation Corps were located on the refuge. The young men built stone houses at refuge headquarters and elsewhere, constructed an extensive irrigation system in the Blitzen Valley, and made many other useful improvements. Today near Page Springs, the Blitzen River is dammed and a large canal skirts each side of the valley. Water from these canals is used to flood extensive meadows, and the excess water returns to the main stream canal (the Blitzen River) and eventually reaches Malheur Lake. In years of excessive runoff, Malheur Lake can overflow by way of Mud Lake into Harney Lake, which is about 10 feet lower. Some people have suggested that this "flushing action" keeps Malheur Lake fresh while Harney Lake is highly saline, if it contains water at all. Because the overflow is extremely dilute and because wind storms transport tons of salt from Harney Lake back into the Malheur drainage, the idea that flushing is essential to Malheur Lake's remaining fresh does not deserve serious consideration. The logistic difficulties in managing such a large area of land are suggested in a refuge pamphlet, which cites 150 miles of dikes, 200 miles of ditches and canals, 200 miles of roads, 450 miles of cattle fence, and numerous dams and flood gates.

At refuge headquarters visitors will find a small museum containing an egg collection, mounted specimens of local birds and mammals, and a selection of literature, including maps, auto tour guides, bird lists, etc. Also, one may inspect the nearby site where the Stenger and Chapman brothers erected a sod house in 1862. The Sod House Springs Pond and trees and shrubbery around headquarters provide excellent birding. Away from headquarters, large sections of the refuge are closed to the public by "Official Use Only" signs. Although special permits may be obtained to enter some of these areas—if valid reasons exist—they are normally open only to refuge employees and grazing permittees. Most visitors are content to travel the Central Patrol Road and other roads open to the public (see Chapter 11).

There is a distinct sequence of seasonal events at Malheur Refuge, and a single visit is like seeing only 5 minutes of a full-length movie. Large flocks of snow geese, white-fronted geese, lesser sandhill cranes, whistling swans, and pintails begin arriving, usually by mid- to late February. These species, best observed off the refuge along Highway 205 between Highway 78 and Wright's Point, will ultimately move farther north to nest. In March, other migratory waterfowl arrive, and the spring migration of waterfowl peaks between mid-March and early April. Most shorebirds reach the area in April, and numbers of passerine birds reach a peak during the last week in April or the first half of May. In late April and May, refuge headquarters and the south end of the Blitzen Valley (e.g., near the P Ranch and Page Springs) are excellent birding spots.

By April some of the larger species, such as Canada geese and greater sandhill cranes, are nesting, and most migrants have moved on northward. Resident nesting species commence courtship activities in mid- or late spring, and many are nesting or have completed nesting by June. By early summer, a dense growth of marsh vegetation begins to interfere with visibility, and more birds may be heard than seen. Through the summer, broods appear and families are raised. Most species of waterfowl develop an eclipse plumage by mid- or late summer, and identification becomes difficult. In late summer, meadows become dry, and many are hayed. Many ducks, geese, and cranes begin to congregate on refuge grainfields, which are planted on a share-crop basis. As fall approaches, species in their southward migration (e.g., whistling swans, ducks, etc.) stop in to feed, but are not easily seen because many use Malheur Lake in years when sago pondweed is abundant. The fall migration peaks in October. By late fall, most migrants have departed, leaving only residents and species that come to the area to winter (e.g., rough-legged hawks).

Deer can be seen anytime on the refuge, but are most apparent in the fall, especially in the Blitzen Valley between Buena Vista and Frenchglen. Muskrats are often seen along the Central Patrol Road. Pronghorns, mink, and porcupine are seen by the lucky few.

Malheur Field Station—About 4 miles west of refuge headquarters is the Malheur Field Station, a facility operated by a consortium of 22 colleges and universities in Oregon and Washington. The station provides dormitory space, meals, and other services and facilities, and is the base of operation for most large groups and many small, private groups that visit southeastern Oregon. During the summer, MFS offers a program of 28 field courses for college credit (e.g., botany, mammalogy, photography, ornithology, geology, archeology, etc.). The station maintains a small research herbarium, a small library, and operates the South Coyote Butte Nature Trail, which gives visitors an excellent orientation to local plants and the high desert region.

Diamond Craters—About 10 miles south of Malheur Lake, along the eastern margin of the Blitzen Valley, is one of Oregon's richest areas of young volcanic activity. Diamond Craters is a natural museum of volcanism including many lava craters, scattered cinder cones, lava flows, complicated systems of lava tubes, and various other features. In places the new unweathered lava appears to have cooled only moments before, and visitors may feel compelled to test it for warmth. The area is isolated—there being no other recent volcanism nearby—about 6 miles in diameter, roughly circular, but easily accessible by car (see Chapter 11). Diamond Craters, a name used since about 1875, refers to the nearby Diamond Ranch where the "diamond" brand was used by Mace McCoy.

The sequence of geological events at Diamond Craters was complicated. Basically, the area is a lava shield composed of lava flows from a central source. Later, the shield was pushed up into domes, pocked with various types of craters, modified by lava flows and violent eruptions, and structurally altered by faulting. What follows is a generalized account of the major circumstances and events, but one should be aware that the story may change drastically with further research.

The original landscape was probably similar to that present

today. The basic rock upon which Diamond Craters rests is a thick deposit (several hundred feet) of stratified siltstones, sandstones, and other material belonging to the Danforth Formation (Pliocene). Although other geologic formations can be found nearby, these did not enter into the formation of Diamond Craters. The story began when lavas from a deep reservoir of magma penetrated the overlying Danforth Formation, spilled out on the surface, and flowed out in all directions to form the basic shield. The ropy lava (pahoehoe) was 75 to 100 feet thick near the center of the shield and thinned to a foot or so at the edge. Toward the end of the eruption, large amounts of the lava drained back into the earth in lava tubes, causing portions of the shield's crust to collapse and leaving a topography of alternating elevations and depressions. Later magma again surged upward into the Danforth Formation, but instead of spilling on the surface, the magma spread horizontally between layers of the Danforth rocks. The magma forced into these layers formed prisms (lacoliths) that pushed upward to form three large domes along a fissure trending northwest-southeast across the shield.

Next came a period of catastrophic eruptions—gas, steam, and lava—and large numbers of craters of various kinds, sizes, and shapes were formed on the surface of the shield. In time, many of these, especially the lava craters, were enlarged as abrupt edges collapsed inward. Many of the cinder cones have gentle slopes formed of diverse ejected material such as ash, rock fragments, and volcanic bombs. Many of these bombs are cored bombs, apparently formed when a fragment of rock was coated with lava, hurled in the air by escaping gas or steam, cooled, and often dropped into molten lava for the process to be repeated. Some cored bombs are pea sized, but others are 2 feet in diameter. Malheur Maar, a crater formed near the western edge of the shield by a steam explosion, contains a pond and is of considerable interest to biologists.

Next came a period of additional doming and violent eruptions of ash and rock near the position of the original central vent. There were more lava flows, and another surge of magma and dome building. When the magma receded, portions of the dome roof collapsed or fell to form grabens. Spatter cones and lava pools formed, and in many of the lava pools, the lava retreated leaving only a crust. Near the southeastern edge of the original shield, a new lava flow covered about 1½ square miles. There were later magma intrusions creating powerful stresses in the northeastern quarter of the shield, where a large series of cracks or fissures may be as much as 15 feet wide and 50 feet deep. Finally, there have been other major sporadic eruptions.

Lava flows from Diamond Craters diverted Riddle Creek from its original course to the Blitzen River and caused the stream to flow into Barton Lake. Although visitors will see no fumaroles or hot springs at Diamond Craters, the area may have geothermal potential because of the underlying magma chamber. The Bureau of Land Management plans to designate Diamond Craters as a natural area. Diamond Craters deserves special consideration, not only because of its geology, but also because of a rich and interesting assemblage of plants and animals. A population of melanistic Western fence lizards lives on the black lavas at Diamond Craters, illustrating the concept of adaptive coloration.

Steens Mountain—One of Oregon's highest (9,733 feet) and most scenic fault-block mountains was called Snow Mountain from 1831 to 1860, when it was renamed after Major Enoch Steen. Today the mountain is a popular vacation land and an excellent out-of-doors nature laboratory. About 76% of the mountain's area is controlled by the Bureau of Land Management and is designated as Recreation Lands, and except for minor parcels of state land, the remainder, including most stream valleys, is privately owned. Steens Mountain is unique among Oregon mountains in that automobiles can be driven right to the summit, where everyone can share the breath-taking view. Because the road is a car killer, visitors are advised to walk from the main loop road.

Steens Mountain offers some excellent examples of glacial topography. Also, the mountain is famous for its incredible displays of colorful wildflowers, which advance with the coming summer from the sagebrush zone up through the juniper belt, aspen belt, and finally to the wind-swept bunchgrass area near the summit. A diverse fauna includes bighorn sheep, pronghorns, deer, marmots, various ground squirrels, many raptors, and other birds. Herds of feral horses are often sighted, especially between Highway 205 and Blitzen Crossing on the Steens Loop road. Steens Mountain is still grazed by cattle, but recreation, photography, hunting, and fishing are rapidly becoming more important uses of the area's resources. Public campgrounds are provided by the BLM at Page Springs, Fish Lake, Jackman Park, and Blitzen Crossing (see Chapter 11).

Hart Mountain National Antelope Refuge—Because of poor roads and isolation from densely populated areas, the refuge is known to only a few people and is not heavily visited. But Hart Mountain is a delightful place and well worth the hardship of getting there. The refuge was established in 1936 for the benefit of remnant herds of pronghorns, but today is concerned with the management of all natural resources found on the vast holding of 275,000 acres.

The refuge straddles Hart Mountain, a scenic fault-block, and includes a remarkable mix of environments ranging from the wind-swept summit of Warner Peak (8,065 feet) to the greasewood flats, alkaline lakes, and dunes of the Warner Valley about 3,600 feet below. Imposing rims, colorful rock formations, steep gorges, and other inspiring scenery are exposed along the west face (scarp) of Hart Mountain. Numerous hot and cold springs, streams, and lush meadows dot the higher terrain.

Fishing is permitted in certain streams, and the refuge occasionally sponsors special hunting seasons in which the quality of the experience is emphasized (e.g., archery, black-powered rifles, etc.). Rock collecting is permitted, but closely regulated. Cattle are grazed according to a permit system, and refuge literature explains that only excess forage is used and that wildlife actually benefits from the grazing! A few public campgrounds and a public bathhouse are available at Hot Springs Campground along Rock Creek, and numerous other campgrounds are open only during hunting seasons. At refuge headquarters, visitors can inspect a small display of native plants and obtain various types of pertinent literature, maps, and other information (Note: the office of the refuge manager is in Lakeview).

Although pronghorns are abundant during the visitor season, the herds move down into the Catlow Valley and other lowlands during winter. Deer, coyotes, sage grouse, many birds of prey, and various other animals are abundant and easily seen. Although bighorn sheep are present, few people see them. Excellent birding is found in riparian vegetation along Rock Creek and in the small grove of ponderosa pine at Blue Sky and Guano Creek. In the Warner Valley, depending upon the season, birding rivals that at Malheur Refuge. The vegetation at Hart Mountain is especially striking, consisting of a mixture of tall and low sage, bitterbrush, snowberry, mountain mahogany, quaking aspen, and many others. Wildflowers create a fantastic display of color in the early summer, and fall colors are often unusually beautiful. See Chapter 11 for road and other information.

The Alvord Basin—Although accustomed to unusual natural beauty and scenic wonders, residents of the Northwest are nevertheless thrilled when first exposed to the Alvord Basin. The Alvord offers a totally different out-of-doors experience. On all sides the basin is walled by mountainous grandeur—the Steens, Pueblos, Trout Creeks, Pine Mountain Range, and several others. Standing at 4,025 feet elevation, one feels humbled, if not intimidated, by the towering summit of the Steens—more than a mile above. Along the scarp of the Steens, abrupt cliffs, rims, and massive pinnacles, formed of layer upon layer of lava, present a remarkable example of sheer ruggedness. And the many hues of the Pueblos, accentuated by shadows and aspen groves and contrasted with the subtle colors of a rich desert flora, can soothe and relax, causing one to set aside trivia that seemed monumental only a moment before. The Alvord Desert, a vast expanse of whiteness, forming one of the largest and most perfect playas in the world, seems to burn lasting images upon the mind. On a bright day, the Alvord Desert is not the place to go without sunglasses. Elsewhere in the basin there are extensive sand dunes, desert pavement, purple hills, marshes, hay meadows, snow-melt streams lined with cottonwoods and willow, and much more.

Also, one can visit quaint hamlets with names such as Fields and Denio. Andrews, Alberson, and Follyfarm are names that persist without being attached to anything particular—history having passed them by. In the Alvord Basin history seems to live, and messages from a former time are strewn about the landscape, providing special reminders of the past. Large cattle spreads, dating back a century or more, are living symbols of the traditional West—solid bastions against an outside world of technology and confusion.

The Alvord has yielded gold, silver, mercury, and borax to a few who were willing to toil and suffer severe hardships. But most of these miners were denied tangible wealth, and had to accept payment for their toil in sunsets, vistas, and serenity. Today a new kind of would-be entrepreneur is dazzled by the area's geothermal resources, but these developers must first subdue Nature and a large number of people who believe that the Alvord Basin is too precious to house steam plants and power lines.

Biologically, the Alvord's affinity is with areas farther south in the Great Basin. Because several desert plants and animals, such as Mormon tea, antelope ground squirrels, and collared lizards reach the northern limits of their distribution in the Alvord Basin, the area is unique. Furthermore, the Alvord is home to some rare and fragile endemics, species that are best served by anonymity. Pronghorns and coyotes may be seen anytime, but deer and bighorn sheep are best seen in winter, when deep snow drives them down to lower elevations. The marshes and lakes, especially in the vicinity of Borax Lake, and the brushy canyons are excellent spots for birding (see Chapter 11).

Large numbers of hunters are attracted to hunt pronghorns and upland game birds, such as chukar, quail, and sage grouse. A limited amount of stream and lake fishing is available. Mann Lake, which has hefty rainbow and cutthroat trout, is a favorite site for fishing through the ice. Thundereggs, agates, and other rocks and minerals make the area popular to rock collectors.

Although a few tourist cabins are available at Fields and Denio, the Alvord Basin has no public camping facilities. Because of the unusual attractiveness of the area, camping facilities are badly needed, not only to accommodate the visitors, but to protect a fragile and beautiful region from unauthorized camping and all the attendant ills.

The Black Rock Desert—South of the Alvord Basin in northwestern Nevada is a huge playa known as the Black Rock Desert. This remote and nearly inaccessible area was formerly a part of Lake Lahontan. The Black Rock Desert extends northward from near Gerlach, Nevada for more than 60 miles, and in the north, is bordered to the east by the Jackson Mountains and to the west by the Calico Mountains. The desert floor is at about 4,000 feet elevation. The Black Rock Range juts southward into the desert and divides it into two northern extensions or forks. The southern-most tip of the Black Rock Range is a 500-foot prominence called Black Rock Point, a conspicuous landmark and the source of the desert's name.

Because the Black Rock Desert is so remote and bleak, it is almost frightening, but is has redeeming beauty that stems from its remote setting and bleak landscape. Vast mud flats of subdued colors, numerous hot springs surrounded by isolated islands of greenery, sand dunes, and mysterious hummocks crowned with desert shrubs punctuate the vast emptiness.

The Applegate Trail, first used in 1846, led northward into Oregon through the Black Rock Desert. This desolate route brought incredible hardship and misery to the thousands of immigrants who chose to travel it. Wagons could barely make it from one water hole to the next, and shade and trees were unthinkable luxuries. Jettisoned belongings littered the route, along which thirst-crazed livestock are said to have plunged into hot springs to a ghastly death. Even today, visitors to the Black Rock Desert should take special precautions: Avoid wet seasons when playas can turn to a quagmire, take plenty of food and water, carry extra gasoline, and inform some responsible person of your planned itinerary.

Malheur Cave—Although Malheur Cave is a few miles outside the Great Basin, it is logically included here because of its proximity and because it is one of Oregon's most popular caves and often visited by tour groups. The cave is about 13 miles east and slightly south of Princeton on the South Fork of the Malheur River (ca. 3 miles off Highway 78). The cave is at about 4,000 feet elevation, and its entrance is located in sagebrush-covered, flat terrain. Surrounded by private land, the cave is the property of the Masonic Lodge of Burns, Oregon.

Malheur Cave is a 3,000-foot lava tube formed in the Pleistocene. The overburden (thickness of the roof) varies from 6 to 20 feet, and the cave floor slopes downward 65 feet in the course of its total length. Ceiling height varies from 8 feet near the entrance to a maximum of 20 feet at a point far back in the cave. An underground lake fills the lower end of the cave, and because the lake level fluctuates about 3 feet annually, the lake rises to within 1,000 feet of the entrance in March and recedes back to about 1,800 feet in October and November. Back about 3,000 feet the lake completely fills the lava tube and is as deep as 23 feet. Divers have gone back another 500 feet to an apparent end of the cave. The cave floor varies in different places, being flat, tilted, or buckled with a central ridge and fissure. In places the ceiling has collapsed, forming large piles of boulders and rubble on the floor.

Although visited by large numbers of people, Malheur Cave is fragile and biologically unique, the home of four endemic species of invertebrates, i.e., a flatworm, an amphipod, an isopod (all aquatic), and a pseudoscorpion. A freshwater fish is occasionally found in the lake, but is not cave adapted and is a species commonly found in adjacent surface waters. No one knows how the fish gets into the cave. Bats, treefrogs, barn swallows, and several invertebrates also use the cave.

Paiute Indians used Malheur Cave as a shelter, and the area surrounding the cave entrance is littered with obsidian flakes. The cave and nearby areas have long since been thoroughly scoured by artifact hunters. In the early 1800's, the Paiutes and Bannocks had a battle at the cave. According to legend, many Paiutes became ill and attributed their bad fortune to some sort of evil doings of a group of Bannocks, who were foraging at Malheur Lake. The Paiutes retaliated by killing all the Bannocks, except one, who was able to return to his tribe in Idaho and report the disaster that had befallen his fellow tribesmen. A war party of Bannocks returned to Malheur, but found that the Paiutes had been alerted (supposedly by coyote) and had taken refuge in Malheur Cave. The cave entrance was barricaded and other fortifications of stone were put in place. The Paiutes held out until winter snows forced the Bannocks to abandon their mission of revenge. The Paiutes remained in the cave until spring. In 1902, when Malheur Cave was first explored by a man named Duncan, parts of the stone barricade were still in place.

Since about 1938, the Masonic Lodge has held their annual meeting in the cave, and in 1950, the cave was deeded to the Burns Lodge. The Masons have built large bleachers and various altars, spread large quantities of wood chips on the cave floor, and altered the entrance so that vehicles can be driven inside. The wood chips pose a serious hazard to the unique animals in the cave. Visitors carry the chips to the lake on muddy shoes, thereby polluting the water and threatening the delicate ecology of this most unusual ecosystem.

Because a flashlight is totally inadequate in the cave, visitors should use a gas lantern. Extra lights should be taken in case one fails. Because the floor is exceedingly slippery and hazardous in places, much care is required to avoid injury. The cave is cool (58 to 62°F), and warm clothes are required. All visitors should exercise care and good ecological ethics so as not to harm the cave or its unique life. Nothing should be collected, turned over, or left behind in the cave. Ellen Benedict of Portland State University and many others have spent years documenting the scientific value of Malheur Cave; all of us should help preserve it.

Wright's Point—About 12 miles south of Burns, Highway 205 crosses a large flat-topped ridge that juts out into the Harney Basin. Named for General George Wright, this conspicuous landmark is a classical example of inverted topography. Wright's Point is 6 miles long and extends into the Harney Basin like a giant finger from a lava-capped mesa located to the west. Wright's Point is about 250 feet high, 600 to 1,800 feet wide, and meanders gently. The nearest lands of equivalent height are Dog Mountain (a nearby tuff ring) and Burns Butte.

Originally, Wright's Point was not a ridge, but the site of a broad, meandering valley, through which a stream flowed in a generally eastward direction. As surrounding uplands eroded, some sedimentary fill was deposited in the valley. Then about 2.4 million years ago, two separate lava flows came down the valley, forming a thick layer of resistant lava over the valley floor. The lava is believed to have originated from vents near Palomino Buttes, west of Wright's Point. During the last 2.4 million years, the surrounding land mass has eroded away, leaving the former valley floor, now protected by a resistant cap of lava, as the top of Wright's Point—250 feet above the surrounding terrain.

Today, cuts made during the construction of Highway 205 expose 200 feet of conglomerates, sedimentary sandstones and mudstones, and volcanic materials deposited on a broad alluvial plain at this site. These deposits have yielded fossil plant remains, fish bones, a pelecypod (i.e., clam-like animal), and a camel tooth. Capping the thick sedimentary deposits are two thin (10 to 30 feet) lava flows, usually touching, but separated in some places by 4 to 6 feet of white volcanic material.

At the eastern tip of Wright's Point, where Camp Wright was once located, the Island Ranch, once owned by John Devine and later by Henry Miller, is currently one of the finest cattle ranches in the Harney Basin.

The Strawberry Mountains—The crest of the Strawberry Range marks the northernmost boundary of the Great Basin. Here a drop of rain can split—half going into the John Day River and ultimately finding its way to the Pacific Ocean, while the other half flows down the Silvies River drainage and ends up landlocked in Malheur Lake. The Strawberry Range is relatively small, but rugged, and has peaks reaching up to 9,038 feet. Higher areas, especially on the northern and eastern exposures, have been lightly glaciated, the main evidence being cirques and short segments of glaciated valleys.

A transect from Malheur Lake to the top of Strawberry Peak involves a gain in elevation of almost a mile and passes through all the typical vegetational zones found on most interior mountains in the West. Beginning in greasewood and saltgrass, one passes through the various coniferous zones to reach subalpine fir, white-barked pine, and finally the treeless zone (see Chapter 11). The mountains support a rich flora, including spectacular displays of wildflowers. The fauna is also diverse and is enriched by many of the typical montane species such as Clark's nutcrackers, jays, pikas, chickarees, voles, etc.

The north side of the Strawberries supported a wild and productive era of gold mining, with 26 million dollars worth of gold extracted at the Canyon City diggings alone. Today the higher parts of the Strawberry Range are included in the Strawberry Mountain Wilderness Area. An excellent system of trails and several beautiful lakes (e.g., High, Slide, and Strawberry) attract many hikers, anglers, and other sight-seers.

At lower elevations, forests and meadows support lumbering and grazing. Hunting is popular, especially for elk, deer, and grouse. The high lakes and many cold streams provide excellent fishing. There are many public campgrounds in the general area.

Because the Strawberry Mountains are part of the Great Basin, and yet so different from typical Great Basin mountains, their educational value is considerably enhanced. The contrast between Steens Mountain and the Strawberries is a worthwhile short course in biology.

There are many other natural history attractions in Oregon's Great Basin country (e.g., numerous caves around Bend, Fort Rock, Hole in the Ground, Abert Lake, The Lost Forest, Silver Lake, Glass Butte, Delintment Lake, to name but a few). We have described only those included in the suggested tours in Chapter 11. It would take a very large book to do justice to all the deserving natural wonders in the northern Great Basin—we had in mind a much smaller book!

Beef wheels, such as this one at the P Ranch,
were used to hang a butchered beef.

Blitzen—one of many abandoned monuments to the failure of homesteaders in the high desert.

Blacktail jackrabbits follow well-worn trails even in snow.

The Malheur Field Station is a center for study of natural resources in southeastern Oregon.

CHAPTER 11

Recommended Tours and Hikes

The tours and hikes recommended here include the obvious ones and do not exhaust the possibilities. There are many little traveled roads and isolated and interesting places awaiting discovery by the curious. To tell all would spoil the fun. We have emphasized the most exciting places in the Harney Basin, but have not ignored noteworthy attractions in adjacent and outlying areas. Features of unusual interest are pointed out, mileages are given, and basic background information is provided. Refer to Chapter 10 when appropriate.

Most tours involve a round trip, and we have attempted to avoid retracing a route, but roads are few, and some repetition is unavoidable. Several tours have optional side trips, and other tours permit through travelers to continue on to another destination. In some instances a tour begins at an intermediate location reached on another tour. This device, while awkward, reduces repetition.

Although the time required to complete a tour is estimated, the actual time will vary depending upon people and their interests. The time estimates assume a liberal amount of sight-seeing. All side trips are extra, and an estimated time is given for each. Round trip distances are given, with side trips being extra and their round trip distances being provided separately. The distance between stops is in parentheses. Using the tour guides requires that you carefully measure distances from one stop to another. Although towns, services, camp sites, and other facilities are sometimes mentioned, the reader should consult Appendix A for more complete information.

Because the Great Basin area is sparsely populated and seldom traveled, visitors should take sensible precautions before traveling. Be sure your car is functioning properly. Carry a spare tire (check its air pressure), a lug wrench, a jack that you can operate, and minimal tools such as pliers, screw driver, and an adjustable wrench. Drive slowly on gravel roads and steer around large rocks—missing the big ones will markedly reduce the number of flats. Keep your gas tank filled and carry plenty of extra water and food. Watch for livestock on roads, especially at night.

Every location has something to offer, so don't rush from one stop to another. Make unscheduled stops, get out, and explore. Watch for wildlife as you travel, but be sure you are safely off the road before stopping to look. Take along appropriate field guides (especially for birds), binoculars, and cameras. Useful maps can be obtained from the Bureau of Land Management and from refuges and other agencies. Please do not disturb wildlife or collect any artifacts or natural materials. Relax and enjoy yourself!

Tour #1

Tour: Headquarters of Malheur Refuge and vicinity.
Route: Malheur Field Station to refuge headquarters, and return by Central Patrol Road.
Estimated Time: 1½ to 3 hours. Morning or evening is best (Note: refuge offices keep business hours).
Distance: 9.7 miles
Hikes: The South Coyote Butte Nature Trail at the Malheur Field Station.
Starting Point: Malheur Field Station

1a— From the Malheur Field Station drive north to the paved county road (1.4). Stands of greasewood, sagebrush, rabbit-brush, and giant wild rye occur along the way. In lowland areas that flood, there are stands of cattail, hard-stemmed bulrush, and other marsh plants. Turn right on the paved road.

1b— Bridge (0.7). Colonies of barn and cliff swallows nest under the bridge. Egrets, great blue herons, waterfowl, and other birds may be seen along the canal. Carp are often visible from the bridge, and common and Western terrestrial garter snakes inhabit the rocks near the base of the bridge. Watch for cars if you stop.

1c— Sod House School (0.35). Grades 1 through 8 are taught in this one-room schoolhouse.

1d— Entrance to the Sod House Ranch (0.1). The road on the right leads to the Sod House Ranch. This ranch was sold to Peter French by a man named Robie in 1877 and became a subheadquarters for French's cattle empire. When French was murdered, 26 December 1897, his body was brought to the Sod House Ranch and later shipped to California. Today the ranch is part of Malheur Refuge, and visitors are welcome. The barn, beef wheel, stone cellar, and remnants of old stockade fences are of historical interest. Notice the "F-G" brand on the cellar door. The large poplar trees were planted in 1892 by Emanuel Clark, French's foreman. Return to 1d and turn right.

1e— Donner und Blitzen River (1.4). The Blitzen originates from snowmelt from Steens Mountain, courses down the Blitzen Valley, and provides essential water for wildlife habitat on the refuge. A few miles from here, it flows into Malheur Lake. In the fall, deer browse the willow thicket near the bridge.

1f— Cinder Pit (0.3). Colonies of bank swallows nest in the walls of the pit; holes mark the entrances to nesting cavities.

1g— Entrance to Visitor Parking Lot (0.2). Refuge headquarters occupies an attractive setting, which was once an Indian camp site. Recent construction has marred much of the natural beauty. The display pond (Sod House Springs) originates from warm springs and attracts many types of waterfowl and shorebirds. Nearby is the original Sod House site, where the first structure in Harney County was built in 1862. Visit the museum and examine the selection of printed matter available to visitors. During office hours, refuge personnel will provide information and assistance. The shrubs and trees at headquarters provide excellent birding, and a large colony of Belding's ground squirrels inhabits adjacent areas. During the summer, the decorative flower gardens may be unusually colorful and a good place to see humming-birds.

SIDE TRIP: Benson Boat Landing (4.6 miles; 30 minutes to an hour). Turn left as you leave the parking lot and left again at the bottom of the hill (0.4). This road crosses the Blitzen River (0.8) and leads to the shore of Malheur Lake near a large grove of willows (1.1). Many kinds of wildlife can be observed along the road. Near the willow grove, watch for great horned owls, red-tailed hawks, and warblers. Muskrats and carp are often active in the nearby water. Return to 1g and resume the tour at the beginning of the Central Patrol Road across from the refuge parking lot.

1h— Proceed onto the Central Patrol Road as you leave the parking lot. As you drive across the hill, you have an excellent view of the Blitzen Valley and Steens Mountain. Deer and coyotes are often seen in the meadows along the right side of the road.

1i— Blitzen River (2.3). After crossing the Blitzen, you pass through a section of marsh, ponds, ditches, and pools that offer some of the best birding on the refuge. Watch for herons, egrets, grebes, ducks, geese, swans, blackbirds, cranes, and many others.

1j— Road Junction (1.7). Turn right to return to the Field Station (1.2) or continue for a tour of the Blitzen Valley (see 3a of Tour #3).

Tour #2

Tour: Cole Island Dike

Route: Refuge headquarters to the end of the dike road and return.

Estimated Time: Two or three hours. Early morning or late evening is best.

Distance: 16.4 miles

Hikes: You may wish to park and walk a portion of the dike.

Starting Point: Visitor parking lot at refuge headquarters. (**Warning:** This tour is for birding and wildlife observation only. The road is impassable when wet and is bad even when dry. Many cars will high center, paint will be scratched, and there are few safe places to turn around).

2a— From the visitor parking lot, travel eastward (toward Princeton) to the Cole Island Dike road (2.1).

2b— The Dike Road (on the left) is 6.3 miles long (read the above warning before taking this road). Cole Island Dike was built in 1936-38, but in 1948, it was ruptured in several places by wave action. The dike is the primary public access to Malheur Lake and, at times, is one of the richest areas for birding (e.g., white pelicans, shorebirds, waterfowl, large waders, birds of prey, etc.). The dike road enables the visitor to see the nature of the expansive freshwater marsh that is Malheur Lake. In early morning, the sounds of the marsh are especially impressive. Deer, muskrats, and coyotes are often seen. Inspect the area carefully before attempting to turn around. If you get stuck, it's a long walk back!

Tour #3

Tour: Blitzen Valley

Route: Refuge headquarters to Frenchglen and return. Note: The refuge's self-guided auto tour follows the same route.

Estimated Time: 4 to 8 hours

Distance: 78 miles

Hikes: Up the Blitzen River from Page Springs, up Krumbo Creek from Krumbo Reservoir, or park and walk up to Buena Vista Overlook.

Starting Point: Refuge headquarters—take the Central Patrol Road (1h to 1j in Tour #1) and begin; Malheur Field Station—drive south 1.2 miles to the Central Patrol Road and begin.

3a— Junction of the Central Patrol Road (CPR) and Malheur Field Station road. Driving south on CPR, you pass through an extensive area of mixed plant types, including willow, hard-stemmed bulrush, cattail, burreed, and others in the lowlands, and greasewood, rabbitbrush, sagebrush, and giant wild rye on higher ground. Irrigated meadows, ponds, and barrow pits are inhabited by large numbers of waterfowl and marshbirds. Deer, coyotes, and antelope may be seen. Drive slowly and watch carefully. Do not stop in the middle of the road.

3b— Canoe Take-out Road (0.5). A canoe trail follows the Blitzen River from near 3e to the end of this road. The canoe trail is recommended only during high water, and even then, high banks obscure view of the surrounding landscape.

3 c— Peter French Murder Site (1.1). About a quarter mile west of here, French was shot by Ed Oliver on 26 December 1897. Saddle Butte is ahead on the right.

3d— McLaughlin Slough (3.9). This old channel of the Blitzen River is an excellent place to see cormorants and many other birds. Rattlesnake Butte is ahead on the left.

3e— Blitzen River (1.6). The canoe trail begins just downstream from the bridge.

3f— Busse Dam (0.5). This dam is one of the many structures in the refuge's complex irrigation system. Without proper water distribution, much of the refuge would be desert shrubland.

3g— Desert Shrubs (0.2). Budsage is among the desert plants growing here. Budsage bears leaves early and drops them when the weather becomes hot and dry. The short, spiny plants appear to be dead during dormancy. The taller plants are greasewood.

3h— Great Horned Owls (2.7). Carefully inspect the willows across the river for owls. If you remain quietly in your car, owls will usually remain perched. Watch for beaver cuttings on willows along the river banks.

3i— Grainfields (1.2). Across the river, huge fields of grain are planted for cranes and waterfowl. Local people farm the land for a share of the crop. Many birds congregate on grainfields during late summer, fall, and early spring.

3j— Buena Vista Road (1.0). After turning right, check the large grainfield (0.2) for geese and cranes.

3k— Buena Vista Pond (0.7). During most seasons, this large, man-made pond is heavily used by large numbers of birds, e.g., grebes, ducks, geese, swans, pelicans, egrets, herons, etc.

3l— Buena Vista (0.9). Currently a refuge substation, this site was once a subheadquarters in Peter French's system of ranches.

3m—Road to Buena Vista Overlook (0.1). Turn left and proceed to the parking area at the summit (0.8). The vantage point of BV Overlook provides a spectacular view of Buena Vista Pond, the Blitzen Valley, and Steens Mountain. Deer and other wildlife can often be seen. Western fence lizards and side-blotched lizards inhabit the crevices in the volcanic rocks along the top of the hill. Colorful crustose lichens grow on many rocks, and obsidian nodules are exposed in some of the large rock faces. BV Overlook is an excellent place for lunch, but children and pets should be closely supervised. Return to 3m and turn left.

3n— Highway 205 (0.2). Turn left to continue the Blitzen Valley tour or to reach the starting point for the Diamond Craters and Round Barn tour. Turn right to return to the Malheur Field Station (19.7) or to Burns (41.0).

3o— Diamond Lane (2.0). The Diamond Craters tour (Tour #4) begins here. Stay on Highway 205 to continue the Blitzen Valley tour.

3p— Grain Camp (1.4). An excellent spot to see sandhill cranes and deer, especially in the fall. As you proceed, note the rims of columnar basalt on both sides of the valley. How was this valley formed?

3q— Rimrocks and Indian Shelter (2.3). Rimrocks are home to chukars, marmots, woodrats, bobcats, and many others, including an occasional golden eagle. Indians once used many of the caves as shelter. Up the hill is a shelter that has been partially excavated by archeologists. Note the smoke-blackened ceiling, grinding mortars, and obsidian flakes. Watch for rattlesnakes, and do not disturb the site.

3r— Krumbo Road (2.8). After turning left, inspect the adjacent ponds for trumpeter swans, egrets, geese, and other birds. The grove of trees at the nearby site of a former ranch is good birding; Northern orioles often nest there.

3s— Blitzen River (0.3). Across the bridge, turn right onto the Central Patrol Road to continue the tour. Go straight for the Krumbo Reservoir side trip.

SIDE TRIP: Krumbo Reservoir (7.4 miles; 1-1½ hours).
On the left (1.4) is Krumbo Pond, a man-made brood pond for waterfowl and a popular resting and feeding place for migratory

birds. Ahead is the Krumbo Valley, an important waterfowl nesting area and winter range for large numbers of deer. On the right side of the road (0.8) is a large boulder inscribed with petroglyphs. The message is not understood—so feel free to make your own interpretations. Krumbo Reservoir (1.4) was built in 1957 for irrigation of the Krumbo Valley. The 200-acre lake supports excellent populations of rainbow trout and large-mouthed bass. Motor boats are prohibited. Cormorants, eared grebes, and many other birds use the reservoir. This is a good place to see eagles. Return to 3s and turn left.

3t— Benson Pond (1.0). Here is one of the nicest spots on the refuge—another good place to eat lunch. The large willows and grove of various shade trees attract many small birds, great horned owls, and others. Beavers have felled many large trees along the water's edge, and there is other evidence of these industrious rodents. In Benson Pond, man-made hummocks project from the water. These "artificial muskrat houses" are used as nesting sites by Canada geese. As you leave Benson Pond and continue on the CPR, you will drive along the Blitzen River and pass through several miles of rich and varied wildlife habitat. Careful observation will be well rewarded.

3u— Bridge Creek (6.8). Fishing is permitted in the Blitzen River upstream from this point. As you travel to the next stop, notice the vigorous stands of Great Basin wild rye.

3v— Willows and Meadows (1.1). This area of interspersed willow thickets, rye and sagebrush-covered uplands, and native meadows is a major nesting area for many birds. Beavers, porcupines, coyotes, and deer may be seen.

3w— P Ranch (1.5). When Peter French came to the Blitzen Valley, he built his headquarters ranch here. The P Ranch, named for the "P" brand that French bought from a man named Porter, became the center of French's rapidly expanding operation. Today the P Ranch is a refuge substation, but the chimney of French's house, which burned in 1948, still stands. Several other historically important structures remain. The beef wheel was used to hang butchered beef to cool, and it provided enough mechanical advantage so that one person could raise a heavy carcass beyond the reach of prowling coyotes and dogs. See if you can figure out how it operates. The willow corrals (restored) reflect considerable ingenuity in the absence of a nearby lumber supply. The Long Barn is typical of the many fine barns built by French. Examine the hinges on the large doors and admire the large junipers that were brought down from Steens Mountain to support the building. The large tower, originally used as a fire tower, now serves as a communal vulture roost. Actually turkey vultures begin arriving at the tower about two hours before sunset. They preen and watch the sunset, at which time they move to the large grove of trees. More than 100 have been seen on the tower. Songbirds, quail, hawks, and owls are commonly seen in the area. Return to the Central Road and turn right.

3x— Steens Mountain Loop Road (0.2). Turn right to complete the tour or left for the side trip to Page Springs.

SIDE TRIP: Page Springs Campground (3.8 miles; 1 hour).
On the right are some nice waterfowl ponds (0.8) and the entrance to Camper Corral (0.6), a private camping facility. At the Blitzen River bridge (0.1), you will see the Page Springs Dam, a major structure in the refuge water-control system. Beyond the Blitzen, a road to the left follows the East Canal, which is open to public fishing downstream to Bridge Creek (3.3). Avoid the East Canal road when the ground is wet, and be sure to close all gates. Along the East Canal road you are likely to see beaver sign, porcupines, waterfowl, and many kinds of small birds. The Page Springs road leads to the right, just beyond the East Canal bridge (0.1). Page Springs Campground has springs, rocky rims, willow thickets, juniper groves, river frontage, and several trails. It is an excellent place to camp, fish, or study nature. During the summer, mosquitoes may be fierce, and visitors should watch for rattlesnakes. Return to 3x.

3y— Road to Frenchglen Hot Spring (1.4). Turn right to complete the tour; left for a short side trip to the hot spring.

SIDE TRIP: Frenchglen Hot Spring (1.8 miles; 20 minutes).
Watch for belted kingfishers and other birds. The spring is the former site of the Frenchglen Bathhouse. This area is a rich birding spot, and a pleasant place to spend a few minutes. Return to 3y.

3z— Frenchglen (0.2). Named for Peter French and his partner, Hugh Glenn, this picturesque hamlet reeks of Western atmosphere. Visit the small store and examine the memorabilia attached to the ceiling. The hotel, owned by the state, is a famous landmark. Frenchglen is the starting point for several other tours (6, 7, and 8). Now take Highway 205 to Burns (60 miles) or to the Malheur Field Station (39.4).

Wildlife is abundant along Highway 205, which borders the refuge for many miles. Chukars, quail, golden eagles, and other species are often seen on the steep juniper- and sagebrush-covered slopes along the left side of the road.

3aa—Diamond Lane (17.7). Starting point for Tour #4.

3ab—Buena Vista (2.0).

3ac— Cliff Swallow Colonies (1.3). Watch for the globe-shaped nests of mud on the overhanging cliffs.

3ad—Unit 8 Pond (2.2). An excellent place to see waterfowl and other marsh birds. Several muskrat houses can be seen around the margin of the pond. Saddle Butte is ahead on the right side of the highway.

3ae— Viewpoint (9.7). A good view of the Malheur Lake area and the Malheur Field Station.

3af— Road to the Refuge and Malheur Field Station (1.9) on the right or continue on Highway 205 to Burns (26.0). The gravel piles near this road junction contain many agates and are a popular collecting place.

3ag— Field Station Road (3.2). Turn right for 1.4 miles.

Tour #4

Tour: Diamond Craters and French's Round Barn

Route: From refuge headquarters or Malheur Field Station, through the middle Blitzen Valley, the Diamond Valley, back through the Princeton area.

Estimated Time: 4 to 5 hours

Distance: 55 miles

Hikes: In the craters area, one can walk in many directions to inspect the various volcanic features.

Starting Point: Junction of Diamond Lane and Highway 205, which can be reached by taking Tour #3 to 3o, or by driving 17.1 miles south on Highway 205 from the refuge-field station junction. If Tour #3 is taken to the starting point, additional time will be required.

4a— Follow Diamond Lane, watching for wildlife along the route.

4b— Blitzen River (1.0). Watch for deer, sandhill cranes, and other wildlife in the large fields on the right. For the next few miles the route passes through various types of habitat. Watch for wildlife.

4c— Saltgrass (3.0). Here desert saltgrass grows profusely on an alkali flat. Various shorebirds may be seen near the pool.

4d— Diamond Junction (2.9). Turn left to Diamond Craters; continue straight to take the Diamond Valley loop trip. (Note:

The loop trip is not recommended unless you wish to visit the Diamond Store).

SIDE TRIP: Diamond Valley (13 miles; 30 minutes).
The route circles through ranchlands and the community of Diamond. About 1.4 miles beyond Diamond, keep left to return to the Diamond Craters road.

4e— Junction (1.1). Keep left.
4f— Junction (0.7). The Diamond loop trip returns here, and the edge of the Diamond Craters lava flows is just ahead on the left.
4g— Entrance to Diamond Craters (1.5). Turn left. Notice the abundance of cinders and other volcanic materials.
4h— Craters (0.45). Here on the right is a large lava crater located within a cinder cone. Observe the flow patterns on the floor of the crater and evidence for late withdrawal of lava back into the feeding vent. Orange and chartreuse lichens decorate the walls of the crater, and scattered patches of white represent woodrat urinating stations and places where fledging birds (ravens, owls?) have defecated—the latter spots being messy and streaked. Lichens and mosses are growing on the large slabs of lava, starting a process that will ultimately reduce the rock to soil. Lava tubes, many of them collapsed, were formed where lava spilled over the crater rim. Watch for rattlesnakes and remember that collecting rock specimens is forbidden. See Chapter 10 for details on the geology of Diamond Craters.
4i— More Craters (0.25). Park on the left. Straight ahead is a large pit crater. Along the west side are some excellent examples of lava tubes formed by spilling lava. Within the crater, notice the lichens, woodrat and bird stations, and the extent to which the sides of the crater have fallen in. There is another large crater beyond this one, and if you explore, you will find numerous craters, caves, and large lava tubes. Watch for melanistic Western fence lizards, side-blotched lizards, great horned owls, and wrens.
4j— Cinder Cone (0.5). Please do not drive to the rim. Here large quantities of cinders and other material have been blown out by escaping gases. As activity subsided, smaller craters formed on the floor of the larger crater. Please avoid disturbing plants along the edge of the cone (e.g., stinking monkey flower, blazing stars, skeleton weed, etc.). The center of the Diamond Craters area is atop the higher area, north of the road. Continue, keeping right and then left to reach 4k.

Other craters occur along the right side of the road.

4k— Malheur Maar (3.5). Park on the rise about 300 yards east of the ranch buildings. Walk up the hill. Plants here include greasewood, sagebrush, spiny hopsage, and saltbush. Sagebrush and side-blotched lizards live among the shrubs. Bright patches of orange lichen grow on the bases of many plants. Malheur Maar contains a small pond that is surrounded by zones of emergent vegetation (e.g., phragmites, which resembles bamboo, hard-stemmed bulrush, cattail, etc.). Waterfowl, coots, and other birds frequent this isolated bit of "marsh". Farther up the hill, lava flows have been broken and collapsed with removal of support from beneath them. Return to 4g (4.7) and turn left. As you travel northeast, observe various volcanic features along the roadway.

4l— Road to French's Round Barn (6.7). Read the historical sign.

4m— Round Barn (1.0). Peter French built the barn as a place to train saddle horses. The actual completion date is unknown, but the barn was in use in 1884. The construction is impressive—including the 250 tons of lava stone hauled 8 miles from Diamond Craters and the gigantic center post of juniper brought from Steens Mountain. The barn is about 100 feet in diameter and is covered with nearly 50,000 shingles. Near the top of the center post, a raven has nested for several years—despite the human disturbance. Today the barn is owned by the Oregon Historical Society. French built similar barns at the P Ranch and in Catlow Valley, but the others no longer stand. Return to 4l and turn right.

4n— Barton Lake (2.3). Watch for waterfowl, wading birds, and pronghorns. Riddle Mountain (elevation 6,356 feet) is beyond. The Diamond lava flows diverted Riddle Creek to Barton Lake. Ahead, you pass through several miles of burned rangeland, much of it now seeded with crested wheatgrass.

4o— Princeton-Malheur Refuge Junction (8.3). Turn left to return to the refuge; right for a side trip to Princeton.

SIDE TRIP: Princeton (6.4 miles; 20 minutes).
The current town of Princeton is the second or third town by that name to be located in the area and is sometimes called New Princeton. The post office opened in 1910. From Princeton you can take Highway 78 north to Burns (38) or south to Winnemucca (183)—or return to 4o and Malheur Refuge.

4p— Irrigated Land (0.8). Near Princeton arid land is being rapidly cleared and irrigated with water from wells. Grain and alfalfa are grown.

4q— Range Fire (0.9). When large tracts of range burn, the BLM seeds the burns with crested wheatgrass for cattle forage. For the next 2 or 3 miles, watch for pronghorns.

4r— Malheur Lake (5.4). Portions of the vast marsh can be seen, with the Blue Mountains in the distance.

4s— Alkali (1.5). Here salt accumulations create such a harsh environment that only greasewood can grow.

4t— Cole Island Dike Road (1.3). See Tour #2.

4u— Refuge Headquarters (2.1). See 1g, Tour #1, and Chapter 10.

4v— Malheur Field Station Road (3.0). Turn left to the field station (1.4) or continue straight to Highway 205 (3.2).

Tour #5

Tour: Harney Lake and the Double O Country

Route: Refuge headquarters or Malheur Field Station to the Narrows and on to the Double O Station, with an optional through trip, loop trip, or return by the same route.

Estimated Time: 3 to 5 hours

Distance: 65 miles

Hikes: Exploration of Harney Lake dunes or walk the Martha's Lake road north of the Double O Station.

Starting Point: Malheur Field Station

5a— Drive north to the paved county road (1.4) and turn left (west). Those coming from refuge headquarters will begin the tour here.

5b— Crested Wheatgrass Seeding (2.3). Sagebrush and other shrubs were killed with herbicide and the area was seeded with crested wheatgrass for cattle forage. The resulting monoculture is not attractive to wildlife, except for certain small rodents.

5c— Agates (0.6). Many people collect agates and other interesting rocks from these gravel pits.

5d— Sacrifice Area (0.15). During hot weather, cattle remain near water all day and graze outward each evening as the temperature cools. The area surrounding water holes soon becomes trampled and devoid of vegetation, while forage far from the water is inadequately grazed.

5e— Highway 205 (0.15). Turn right. As you drive, notice the orange lichens on the larger stems of greasewood.

5f— Narrows (1.4). A lively town, with a store, hotel, post office, etc., existed here for many years. A few old buildings remain. In 1889, a post office named Springer was opened, but in 1892, the name of the community was changed to Narrows. Although only a ranch now occupies the site, some mail still arrives addressed to Narrows.

5g— Narrows Bridge (0.3). In exceptionally wet years, water from Malheur Lake spills over, flows through this narrow channel (east to west) into Mud Lake, and may even reach Harney Lake. The marshes on either side of the road are among the most productive bird-watching areas on Malheur Refuge. Colonies of cliff and barn swallows build mud nests on the undergirders of the bridge. On hot days, asphalt may drip into the nests, fowl feathers of adults, and kill large numbers of nestlings. Barn swallows build a cup-shaped nest; cliff swallows construct a globe with a single entrance hole. An earlier bridge was located near the tree on the left.

5h— Double O Road (1.0). Turn left. As you drive through the saltbush, rabbitbrush, sagebrush, and greasewood, watch for pronghorns, sage thrashers, and jackrabbits. Dog Mountain and Wright's Point are on the right; the conical peak a-head in the distance is Iron Mountain (elevation 5,367).

5i— Pictographs (5.0). Turn right and drive to the parking area near the base of the cliffs (0.2). Inspect the pictographs drawn with red pigment on the cliff surfaces. One drawing seems to depict a 6-legged lizard. Please do not touch the pictographs. Obsidian flakes in the area suggest that this site may have been used several thousand years ago when Harney Lake was a large freshwater lake. Note the raven nest on the cliff and the streaks left by the fledglings as they perched for several days after leaving the nest. **Rattlesnakes den in these cliffs, so be watchful.** Note the hopsage (reddish bark with white stripes). Return to 5i.

5j— Road to Dunes (0.45). Turn left. **Warning:** When wet this road is muddy; when dry, it has deep alkali dust, and roadside greasewood plants will ruin a good paint job. Park at the end of the road (1.0). You may see sagebrush lizards (or tracks) in the nearby shrubs. From the top of the dunes, you get an excellent view of Harney Lake. Ordinarily, the lake is a dry, salt-encrusted playa, although it may contain shallow water during the spring. About 2 miles south along the dunes is a place called Sandgap, where overflow from Mud Lake flows into Harney Lake. Peter Skeene Ogden crossed the gap in 1826, as did Peter French and others who were fleeing from Indians in 1878. Far out on the playa are "islands", formed where springs emerge and are surrounded by vegetation. Mirages and dust devils are often visible on the playa. On the dunes, wind has blown the sand away from the root systems of greasewood plants, leaving grotesque hummocks and intricate patterns of cross-bedded sand. Harney Lake is set aside as a natural area—nothing should be collected or disturbed. Do not try to drive on the dunes. Watch for animal tracks in the sand and notice how the dune system spreads and eventually becomes stabilized by invading plants. Return to 5j.

5k— Dunes (2.2). If you did not drive to the dunes at 5j, park, and walk to them here.

5l— Playa (0.4). Because of salt deposits and standing water in the springtime, few plants other than greasewood are able to survive on this playa.

5m— Playa (3.2). Here, a playa has more salt deposits and nothing is able to invade it, although desert saltgrass grows to the edge and greasewood occurs on higher ground. The nearby dunes are old and nearly stabilized. As you continue, watch for waterfowl and other wildlife.

5n— Junction to U.S. 20 (3.1). Turn right to U.S. 20 (21), Riley, and points west. To continue tour, go straight.

5o— Silver Creek (0.1). This stream originates in the Ochoco National Forest, flows past Riley to Moon Reservoir, and eventually reaches Harney Lake. Flow is minimal, except during spring runoff.

5p— South Harney Road (0.05). It is possible to turn left here and circle Harney Lake to Highway 205 at 5e. For several miles, one sees marshes, ponds, and excellent wildlife habitat. Later the road passes under rocky rims and through desert vegetation. Golden eagles, pronghorns, and other wildlife can be seen. Although this route is interesting, **it should not be attempted after rains or after a long period of dry weather**. Portions of the road may have alkali dust 6-8 inches deep—enough to clog air filters and actually stop a car. The road is infrequently traveled, and it is a long walk to assistance. As you continue the tour, your route passes through wetlands. Note the cattails, hard-stemmed bulrush, rushes, and other marsh plants. Watch for wildlife.

5q— Double O Station (4.1). Turn left to the former site of the Double O Ranch. The Double O Ranch was established in 1875, and the first set of buildings was destroyed during the Indian uprising of 1878. Afterward, new buildings were built, including the blacksmith shop and log house that still stand. Today, the Double O is a refuge substation. Across from the Double O is the Martha's Lake road which leads through marshlands and past ponds for 1.3 miles. This area is excellent birding. Many people will want to end the tour at the Double O station and return to 5h.

5r— Warm Springs Creek (0.5). The water flowing through the culvert originates from some large springs just south of here. The springs were a favorite Indian camp site. You may see large carp in the stream.

5s— Road to Martha's and Derrick Lakes (0.55). This road (on the right) is closed to vehicles but walking is permitted outside of the nesting season. The road leads to Martha's Lake, and on to Derrick Lake. These lakes are heavily used by waterfowl (e.g., snow geese) during the spring migration and are important nesting sites during the summer for many species. Beyond Derrick Lake is Stinking Lake, a research natural area that is closed to the public. Return to 5h, from where you can turn left to Burns (25 miles) or right to the Malheur Field Station (7.2).

Tour #6

Tour: Steens Mountain
Route: Steens Mountain Loop Road (Note: This road is not usually open until about July 4—inquire at Frenchglen).
Estimated Time: A full day
Distance: 68.6 miles (with no services)
Hikes: Numerous hikes are available including a walk downstream from Fish Lake, a hike into Kiger Gorge (strenuous), a walk to the summit on the East Rim road, or a hike into Wildhorse Lake (strenuous). If you walk, stay on trails and avoid stepping on plants, especially near the top of the mountain.
Starting Point: Frenchglen, which can be reached by driving 60 miles south from Burns on Highway 205, or by taking Tour #3 (36.4).

6a— At the end of Frenchglen's main street, keep left on the gravel road.

6b— Junction (0.2). Turn left. For the next mile watch for cranes, coots, waterfowl, muskrats, and other wildlife.

6c— P Ranch Junction (1.2). Keep right, but if you wish to visit the P Ranch as a side trip, see 3w on Tour #3.

6d— Page Springs Campground Road (1.5).

6e— Entrance to Steens Mountain Recreation Lands (0.5).

6f— Crested Wheatgrass Seeding (0.5). Sagebrush and other shrubs were killed with herbicide, and the area seeded with crested wheatgrass for cattle forage. As you proceed notice the sign giving precautions about Steens Mountain weather.

6g— Juniper Belt (3.3). Here at the lower edge of the juniper belt,

135

the trees are scattered and form an open woodland. Farther up the mountain, junipers become more abundant and, in some places, form a closed canopy. Note that junipers have no distinctive shape. Much of the Steens deer herd winters in the juniper belt, and chipmunks and golden-mantled ground squirrels are abundant in rocky areas.

6h— Quaking Aspen (1.2). Here aspen occurs only on protected or shaded slopes. Better stands are found at higher elevations. Observe the white bark and the vertically flattened leaf petiole, which permits the leaf to "quake" or tremble in the breeze.

6i— Mountain Mahogany (1.3). Examine the trees on the rocky knoll on the left. Mountain mahogany prefers shallow, rocky soil. An awn that curls and uncurls in response to humidity changes is attached to the seed. This mechanism pushes the seed down to the soil, where it has a better chance of germinating and taking root. Oregon grape, snowberry, currant, and other shrubs grow among the junipers here.

6j— Belding's Ground Squirrels (3.0). These ground squirrels are widely distributed on the mountain. A large colony occurs here, and individuals can often be seen basking on the large boulders, which are glacial erratics. Red-tailed hawks, predators of the squirrels, are also abundant.

6k— Dead Quaking Aspen (1.6). This aspen grove was sprayed with herbicide during brush control operations. The spraying of the trees may have been intentional, accidental, or a consequence of drift.

6l— Lily Lake (1.2). This handsome lake is a classic example of vegetative succession, with concentric zones of plants ranging from the most aquatic (e.g., water lily), through rushes, sedges, willows, and terrestrial species such as grasses, shrubs, and aspen. Continued accumulation of dead vegetation and mineral sediments will eventually fill the lake and turn it into a bog (see 6o). Pacific treefrogs, boreal toads, and a rich assemblage of invertebrate life inhabit the lake and its margin. A few pairs of ducks usually nest here, as does a colony of blackbirds. The grove of aspens houses mountain bluebirds, Cassin's finches, and other songbirds, and is an ideal picnicking spot. Although ponderosa pine is not native to Steens Mountain, some enterprising person has planted seedlings around Lily Lake, hoping to make the area more useful. If you see any of these introduced seedlings, you will be doing Nature a service by pulling them up!

6m— Fish Lake (1.5). This glacial lake has an attractive setting, surrounded by aspen groves, willows, and a rich flora of shrubs and wildflowers. Fish Lake is the largest and most popular campground on Steens Mountain. The area is excellent for birding, several species of reptiles and amphibians occur around the lake margin, and beavers and muskrats inhabit the lake. Eastern brook, cutthroat, and rainbow trout occur, and the lake is periodically stocked with catchable rainbows. To protect the aspen, the BLM hauls firewood many miles for the use of campers. Down Lake Creek about a mile, one can see a large series of beaver ponds and many types of songbirds.

6n— Pate Lake (0.3). Private.

6o— Whorehouse Meadows (0.7). This former site of a shallow lake has filled in to form a bog. The willows and aspen provide excellent birding. At one time this area was home to the sheepherders who tended bands of sheep on the mountain. They carved some of their fantasies, many of which are quite obscene, in the bark of certain aspens.

6p— Honeymoon Lake (0.3). Private.

6q— Fish Creek Viewpoint (0.7). A nice view of a glaciated valley and the adjacent countryside.

6r— Jackman Park (0.05). Here is a small, fragile campground surrounded by aspen groves and meadows of false hellebore, willows, and various wildflowers. Jackman Park is a good place to see several species of small birds. Because this site is so fragile, please avoid camping here.

6s— Kiger Viewpoint Road (4.0). Park large cars with low clearance and walk. You may see marmots, horned larks, sage grouse, hawks, and other wildlife along the way. From Kiger Viewpoint, one sees a natural spectacle, whose excellence is matched in few places in the West. You stand atop a shear wall at the head of a glacial cirque and look out over one of the most perfect glacial valleys in existence. One can easily imagine the valley filled with a creeping valley glacier. Across the valley is Big Nick, a col that is a familiar landmark visible for 100 or more miles in several directions. The pebbly surface of the ground (felsenmeer) is fragile and dotted with stunted alpine flowers, such as lupine and buckwheat. It is a sin to even touch these delicate plants. If you sit down and watch, violet-green swallows and kestrels may cruise by, and after some intense inspection, you may be able to locate deer far below in the valley or along the steep valley walls. If you are lucky, a hummingbird may visit. A short walk to the right reveals the main glaciated canyon; to the left, perhaps a half a mile, a crude and steep trail leads down into the gorge. Keep close watch on pets and children, and do not throw or roll rocks. In the distance, you can see the Blitzen Valley and identify many landmarks (e.g., Harney Lake)—if you know where to look. Also, find the Catlow Valley and Hart Mountain beyond. With a map, many geographic features can be identified. Return to 6s.

6t— Little Blitzen Gorge (1.7). Standing atop the wall of the cirque, one gets a splendid view of this glaciated valley. Small cirques along the edge of the main valley form hanging valleys, and streams tumble from some, down the cliffs to the main valley below. Red-tailed hawks or even prairie falcons may be seen soaring over the gorge.

6u— Road to East Rim Viewpoint (1.2). This road is not good— you may elect to walk.

6v— East Rim Viewpoint (0.4). Be prepared for a breath-taking view. A mile below is the Alvord Desert, with Coyote Lake and other large playas in the distance. Several mountain ranges can be identified around the Alvord Basin (e.g., Trout Creek Range, Pueblos, etc.). Looking north along the crest of the Steens, you can see Mann, Juniper, and Fifteen Cent lakes. On the incredibly rugged scarp, dozens of layers of Steens Basalt are visible, with vertical dikes cutting through the ridges here and there. Just below the East Rim, small valley glaciers have formed cirques, many of which contain shallow lakes or jewel-like meadows. These cirques are favored by bighorn sheep. Below the cirques, intensive erosion has cut V-shaped canyons that lead down to fans along the edge of the Alvord Basin. The Alvord Ranch is directly below among the grove of trees. Notice the colorful hues of lichens on the nearby lava cliffs. White-throated swifts, violet-green swallows, kestrels, ravens, and other birds may glide by, and golden eagles are sometimes spotted soaring high above the desert floor. Again, please avoid damaging delicate alpine plants, watch children, and avoid throwing or rolling rocks. Return to 6u.

6w— Wildhorse Lake Road (0.05). Because this road is **dangerous and nearly impassable**, new model cars having low clearance should not be taken on it. If time permits, you may wish to walk or drive part way and then walk. Keep on the road.

SIDE TRIP: Wildhorse Viewpoint and Summit (3.8 miles, 1 hour). The road leads past the head of Big Indian Gorge and provides a superb view of hanging valleys along the south rim of the gorge. Near the top, at the parking area, the rocky soil supports fragile plants, some of which are scientifically unique. This area was designated as a natural area until 1977 and deserves your special care and consideration. On the left is a beautiful cirque, and on the right, a road (**not to be driven**) leads to the head of the Wildhorse Lake cirque. Walking up toward the radio facility, you get an excellent view of Wildhorse Lake, the south end of the Alvord Basin (Alvord Lake, Fields, Pueblos, etc.), the vast region of the low Steens (i.e., Smith Flat), the Catlow Valley, and other landscape. This is the highest point that can be reached by car in Oregon (it has to be a fantastic car). There is a poor trail to Wildhorse Lake, beginning near the head of the cirque, but the hike is strenuous and dangerous. The lake is populated with cutthroat trout. Return to 6w.

6x— Glaciation (0.4). Glacially polished rocks are visible here. As you proceed, watch for marmots, Belding ground squirrels, hawks, and other wildlife.

6y— Red Snow (0.7). A red-pigmented alga (actually a species of green alga) imparts the red hue to these snowfields.

6z— Glacial Erratics (2.4). The large boulder on your right has been transported and stranded by glacial ice. From this point the road follows a ridge between Big Indian Gorge on the left and the Little Blitzen Gorge on the right. Watch carefully for wildlife.

6aa—Viewpoint (2.9).

6ab—Woodrats (0.3). Note the white patches on the nearby cliffs designating urinating stations.

6ac—Blitzen Gorge Viewpoint (0.7). Examine the numerous lava flows exposed on the opposite wall of the canyon. Nearby are many colorful patches of lichens and more woodrat stations.

6ad—Big Indian Gorge (0.3). Here is a photogenic view of the gorge's length. The land at the bottom is privately owned, as is most of the bottom land in the Steens Mountain gorges. On the right is Little Indian Gorge. Notice that you have returned to the juniper belt, and that mountain mahogany is abundant. Watch for deer.

6ae—Low Steens (0.3). The large flat region below is the low Steens, which contrast sharply with the high Steens. The precipitous separation is the result of a vertical displacement along a major fault. Smaller faults in the low Steens have produced a strange and complicated pattern of parallel drainages.

6af— Moraines (3.0). Large systems of moraines are absent near the mouths of most glacial valleys on Steens Mountain. Apparently the debris has been washed away by glacial melt waters. Here portions of the moraines are still intact, and some huge glacial erratics can be seen, especially on the north side of the road.

6ag—Blitzen Crossing (3.2). This small campground is an excellent site for seeing songbirds and small mammals. Fishing is sometimes quite good, especially downstream. Watch for rattlesnakes along the stream.

6ah—Feral Horses and Pronghorns (2.2). For the next several miles watch for horses, pronghorns, and other wildlife.

6ai—Intermittent Streams (2.1). In the high desert area, many streams flow for only part of the year. Overgrazing of watersheds hastens runoff and reduces the period of flow.

6aj—Desert Water Hole (8.0). A good place to see shorebirds, waterfowl, and game.

6ak—Highway 205 (5.1). Turn right to Frenchglen, or left to Fields (see 8d, Tour #8).

6al—Hart Mountain Refuge Road (3.1). See 7c, Tour #7—but check your gas gauge!

6am—Rock Fence (5.2). Before barbed wire was readily available, many rock fences were built. Peter French built this one to control cattle movement between the Catlow and Blitzen valleys. Catlow Lake, a pluvial lake that once occupied Catlow Valley, may have found an outlet into the Harney Basin through this narrow canyon. Although ichthyologists have suggested this possibility, geologists have found no evidence to support the idea.

6an—Blitzen Valley (0.7). Here one is treated to a panoramic view of the Blitzen Valley, Steens, Jackass Mountains, etc. Note the P Ranch and the pattern of different types of marsh vegetation in the valley. Frenchglen is below.

6ao—Frenchglen (1.2). From here return to Burns (60) or the Malheur Field Station (39.4).

Tour #7

Tour: Hart Mountain Antelope Refuge and Warner Valley.
Route: Frenchglen to Hart Mountain Refuge and return.
Estimated Time: A full day, or preferably two days.
Distance: 107.6 miles (no services except at Plush)
Hikes: Many are possible, e.g., Hot Springs Campground to Warner Peak, to the summit of Hart Mountain (Warner Valley overlook), or along the road to Blue Sky Hotel (i.e., down Guano Creek).
Starting Point: Frenchglen, which can be reached by driving 60 miles south from Burns on Highway 205, or by taking Tour

#3 (36.4).

7a— Follow Highway 205 out of Frenchglen. Climbing out of the Blitzen Valley, you will enjoy a spectacular view.

7b— Rock Fence (1.7). This rock fence, built by Peter French when barbed wire was not readily available, controlled movement of cattle between the Blitzen and Catlow valleys.

7c— Hart Mountain Refuge Road (5.2). Although this road begins as an all weather road, it degenerates to a mere rocky path in places. Be well provisioned and expect to meet few travelers. If you are not properly prepared, consider taking the Alvord Basin trip (see 8c, Tour #8). Watch for golden eagles and other wildlife, especially horned larks in the road.

7d— Feral Horses and Pronghorns (16.0). Driving through the open desert, watch for feral horses, pronghorns, deer, coyotes, jackrabbits, and other animals.

7e— Rock Creek Reservoir (4.1). This isolated body of water is a good place to see waterfowl, wading birds, deer, pronghorns, and other wildlife. The reservoir is stocked with rainbow trout and crappies.

7f— Beaty Butte (3.6) The large conical volcano (elevation 7,916 feet) on the left is a conspicuous landmark named by Colonel C.S. Drew for Sergeant A.M. Beaty. A paleontological site on the flanks of the butte has yielded a rich fauna of Miocene mammals, including primitive dogs, horses, camels, rabbits, and others. Ahead and to the right is Poker Jim Ridge.

7g— Flook Lake (12.0). This large playa is typical of many found in the region, especially farther south. The borders of these playas are favored by pronghorns during the spring and early summer. As you continue, watch for sage grouse in the short sagebrush.

7h— Hart Mountain Refuge Headquarters (6.9). Information, maps, and refuge literature are available, and there are small exhibits of refuge animals and native plants. Check refuge regulations governing various activities. From headquarters, you can take a side trip to Plush, a side trip to Blue Sky or Guano Creek (beginning at 7i), or continue to the Hot Springs Campground at 7k. You are likely to see pronghorns, deer, coyotes, sage grouse, and other wildlife along all these routes.

SIDE TRIP: Warner Valley and Plush (48.8 miles; 2-3 hours). Drive west from headquarters watching for wildlife. As you descend into the Warner Valley (3.4), watch for bighorn sheep on the steep slopes around you. Below are Blue Joint Lake, Lower Campbell Lake, and others, including several dry playas and

141

numerous sand dune systems. Dust devils are often visible in the valley below. North along the right side of the Valley (1.1), terraces are clearly visible, marking the former shoreline of the pluvial lake that once occupied Warner Valley. If you do not wish to visit the Plush Store, you may elect to turn back after inspecting the valley floor. If you proceed, the road will follow along the base of the Hart Mountain scarp. Many spectacular and colorful rock formations are exposed. Near Hart Lake (13.4), the road passes through marshes and meadows inhabited by large numbers of waterfowl, marsh birds, and other wildlife. At Plush, you have the option of continuing to Adel (18.0) and taking Highway 140 to Lakeview (33.0) or Winnemucca (184.0), or returning to 7h (24.4). The road to Adel passes Crump and Pelican lakes where you will see a spectacular mix of marsh vegetation, large numbers of waterfowl and pelicans, and conspicuous terraces of the former pluvial lake that filled the basin. The Adel store and bar has a display of pioneer relics and mounted specimens of big game which are worth stopping to see.

7i— Road to Guano Creek and Blue Sky (1.7). Take the side trip to Blue Sky and Guano Creek or continue to the campground at 7k.

SIDE TRIP: Guano Creek and Blue Sky (25.8 miles; 3-4 hours). This side trip takes you through some of the richest upland game habitat in the northern Great Basin. The road passes desert water holes (2.2). a viewpoint (0.9), aspen groves (2.0), mountain mahogany (1.8), burned rangeland (2.0), and other attractions. Note the bitterbrush, giant wild rye, mountain mahogany, and other vegetation. A branching road (southern boundary road) leads south to Highway 140 and passes through some extremely remote country—it should not be traveled by single passenger cars. At Guano Creek, a large grove of isolated ponderosa pines provides an outstanding site for birding and general nature study. Nearby is a facility called Blue Sky Hotel, which is used by the Order of the Antelope—a private organization—for annual meetings. The road continues up Guano Creek through a beautiful canyon and returns to Hot Springs (6.8), passing below Warner Peak, but gates may be locked, and ordinary passenger cars cannot make the trip. Camping along Guano Creek is permitted only during hunting season. The creek is open to fishing. Return to 7i.

7j— Valet Springs (1.6). Only creek water is available at Hot Springs Campground, therefore, visitors must haul drinking water from this spring. As you proceed, notice the mountain mahogany on your right. Bitterbrush appears here in abundance among the sagebrush.

7k— Hot Springs Campground (1.0). Several camp sites, a public bathhouse, and other camping facilities are available. The streamside growth along Rock Creek is inhabited by many types of songbirds, and a large number of beaver ponds occur 1.5 miles downstream. In spring and early summer, the surrounding meadows and hills are brightened by wild iris, cinquefoil, mustards, and other flowering plants. The stream contans red-band trout and is open to public fishing. Several hikes can be taken from the campground. Because the entire area is quite fragile, visitors should use the campground with extreme care. Near the bathhouse, notice the mineral accumulations formed by precipitation of salts from the hot springs. Return to 7c (53.8), where you may return to Frenchglen (6.9) or join Tour #8 at 8c.

Tour #8

Tour: Loop Trip to the Alvord Basin (around the base of Steens Mountain).

Route: Frenchglen, Catlow Valley, Alvord Basin, Princeton and back to the Malheur Refuge.

Estimated Time: A full day

Distance: 175 miles

Hikes: Walking is required to see several of the recommended sites.

Starting Point: Frenchglen, which can be reached by Highway 205 or Tour #3.

8a— Take Highway 205 from Frenchglen. As the road winds upwards, you get a spectacular view of the Blitzen Valley and surrounding mountains.

8b— Rock Fence (1.8). Before barbed wire was readily available, Peter French built this rock fence to control cattle movements between Blitzen and Catlow valleys.

8c— Hart Mountain Refuge Road (5.2). See 7c, Tour #7.

8d— Steens Mountain Loop Road (3.1). See 6ak, Tour #6.

8e— Blitzen Road (2.3). The side trip to Blitzen should not be attempted after rains or late in the summer when alkali dust may be bad.

SIDE TRIP: Ghost Town of Blitzen (16.6 miles; 1-2 hours). Turn right, drive 3.1 miles, bear left for 1.2 miles to a gravel road, and proceed 4.0 miles. Blitzen and several other towns sprang up

in the Catlow Valley early this century when the homestead allotment jumped from 160 to 320 and finally to 640 acres. The town
thrived for a few years of favorable weather, but when dry weather
resumed, agriculture was impossible, and the people began
moving away. Notice how the wind has blown soil and deposited it
around buildings. Also, notice the dead but standing poplars and
lilacs, perfectly preserved in the dry air. Try to decide the
function of each building. Obsidian flakes are scattered about,
suggesting that Indians once resided here, perhaps hunting marsh
birds around the edge of a diminishing Catlow Lake. Today,
kangaroo rats (see the burrows and tracks) and a few cottontails
are the only residents, but one can imagine that Blitzen might have
been a lively place on a Saturday night—back when it was a
growing and hopeful Catlow Valley farming town. Please do not
collect or disturb anything. Return to 8e.

8f— Terraces (0.5). On the left, the ancient shorelines of Catlow
Lake are visible. During glacial times, water filled the Catlow
Valley with a 351-square-mile pluvial lake that was 75 feet
deep (at maximum extent).

8g— Indian hemp (1.2). The large patch of plants on the left is
Indian hemp. Indians twisted fibers of this plant into a remarkably strong but delicate cordage. As you proceed,
notice the large springs and caves on the left. These caves
were occupied by Indians as long ago as 9,000 years—perhaps when Catlow Lake lapped at the doorway. This land is
private, and public entry is not permitted.

8h— Roaring Springs Ranch (0.9). This large ranch is owned by a
corporation and includes extensive holdings in the Catlow
Valley. It was once a part of Peter French's vast cattle
spread.

8i— Home Creek and Home Creek Ranch (8.0). Home Creek
drains a portion of the low Steens. The ranch was established
about 1884 and was owned by the Shirk family.

8j— Three Mile Creek and Ranch (3.7). The creek is short, originating primarily from a series of large springs. The canyon is
excellent birding, and during the spring, red-band trout from
Three Mile Reservoir run up this stream to spawn. The ranch
dates to 1884.

8k— Six-mile Lake (3.0). A nice waterfowl pond. Notice the encroaching dunes.

8l— Beaty Butte (0.7). The conical volcano (elevation 7,916 feet)
on the right across the valley is Beaty Butte, a conspicuous
landmark. A paleontological site on the flanks of the butte
has yielded fossils of many Miocene mammals, including

primitive dogs, horses, camels, rabbits, and others.

8m— Sand dunes (2.5). Here you can drive (to the right) to the dunes and explore them. Watch for leopard lizards, jackrabbits, and kangaroo rats. An abundance of obsidian flakes reveals this locality to be a former Indian camp site. Do not try to drive in the sand.

8n— Skull Creek (2.4). As you proceed, note the terraces and lava rims on the left.

8o— Long Hollow (8.3). Watch for herds of feral horses high on the hills to the left. You may also see pronghorns and golden eagles.

8p— Summit (2.7). On the right are the Pueblo Mountains. Ahead is the Alvord Basin, with the Trout Creek Mountains beyond.

8q— Old Road to Fields (3.0). The road to the right is a seldom used and bumpy road to Fields (2.9). If you take it, watch for antelope ground squirrels and leopard lizards along the last half-mile stretch. On the hill to the left is an abandoned cinnabar (mercury) mine, including a kiln and various kinds of abandoned equipment. There is a road leading to the mine (0.1). **Be very careful and avoid the old mine shaft**. Watch for Western fence lizards.

8r— County Road Junction (2.1). Turn right to Fields and Tour #9, or turn left to continue the tour. Check your gas gauge.

8s— Fields (1.4). Established in 1881 as Field's Station by Charles Fields, the station became a stopping place for travelers and freight haulers. Across the road from the store is a grove of willows that is a good birding site. A walk up the old road behind the store may reveal leopard lizards and antelope ground squirrels. Tour #9 begins at Fields. Return to the north fork of the junction at 8r (1.9) to continue the Alvord Basin tour.

8t— Borax Lake Road (3.2). Turn right near the grove of trees. As you proceed, keep right and watch for desert pavement antelope ground squirrels, and leopard, whiptail, and desert horned lizards.

8u— Soap Lake (2.4). Park near the lake and do not attempt to drive beyond. Soap Lake supports populations of waterfowl, wading birds, and a rare fish—the Alvord chub. Near the parking place, there are many wind-polished nodules of obsidian (Apache teardrops). Inspect the nearby system of largely stabilized sand dunes. If you have **old shoes**, wear them, and do not try to cross wet places by wading barefooted—saltgrass and greasewood penetrate even the toughest skin. Follow the road upward along the small stream. Observe the accumulation of salts on the soil surface, and on the left, examine the old borax vets (see Chapter 8). Near the top of the hill is a sod house, and just beyond is Borax Lake. Minerals from the thermal springs in the lake precipitate to form rock along the lake margin, and the lake margin is gradually "rising" above the surrounding terrain. If you can stand the odor of the mud, take a dip in the warm water. Be careful of walking on saltgrass! Next walk north about a quarter mile and observe a large series of hot springs and glory pools of various sizes, shapes, and temperatures. Avoid the tall vegetation—you may fall in a concealed spring. For the next mile, you will be treated to algae of every hue, steam vents, boiling springs, and eerie pools that seem to extend down to the dark depths of the earth's bowels. As you might imagine, this area is of considerable interest for possible geothermal development. Here you will see the same mineral-deposited rock that was present at Borax Lake. Salt deposits cover the soil, and saltgrass, greasewood, and borax weed are the only plants. Alvord Lake is beyond the last hot spring. Return to your car and to 8t.

8v— Alvord Lake (1.5). Usually a dry playa or a shallow lake (right).

8w— Wildhorse Canyon and Steens Summit (6.9). Visible ahead.

8x— Andrews (1.2). A post office was established here in 1890 and named for Peter Andrews who came to the Wildhorse Valley that same year. The post office functioned until the early 1970's. Andrews has the distinction of receiving the least rainfall of any recorded weather station in Oregon (about 7 inches a year).

8y— Serrano Point (4.6). Here the Alvord Desert (really a large playa) suddenly comes into view.

8z— Frog Springs (1.7). The road to the right leads to a nice spring and patch of willows. Chukars come to the spring to drink, as do many other animals.

8aa—Road to Alvord Desert (1.6). This road leads to the edge of the playa. **Do not** drive on the playa when the surface is wet, and do not drive north where entering streams may turn the playa to a sea of mud. (Note: The surface can be dry, but conceal mud down an inch or two.). Do not race or make sharp turns. You can drive across the desert to inspect the adjacent dunes. Steens Mountain and the desert floor make a picture not soon to be forgotten.

8ab—Bathhouse (1.0). A hot spring emerges near the road on the right. Observe the colorful algae. The water flows to a small bathhouse, which is on private land belonging to the Alvord Ranch (see 8ad). The public had free access to the bathhouse until recently—now permission is required.

8ac— Pike Creek (2.1). The trees and shrubbery along this creek are inhabited by many kinds of birds. A walk up the canyon often reveals chukars, dippers, and other birds. Thundereggs may be found along the way. Watch for lizards.

8ad—Alvord Ranch (3.7). Here on the former site of Camp Alvord (1864-1866) is the Alvord Ranch, established in 1871 as part of John Devine's extensive holdings. When Devine declared bankruptcy, Henry Miller bought out Devine, but retained him to supervise the property. Miller later gave the Alvord Ranch to Devine, who turned it into a showplace of exotic animals and stylish living. The old barn is a historical landmark, and the great ranch continues to be an exciting bit of the old West.

8ae— Fan (2.0). Here at the base of the Steens scarp, collected erosion products from the great lava flows have washed to the mouth of a canyon and spread out to form a fan. Note the vertical gullying.

8af— Road to Mickey Hot Springs (2.8).

SIDE TRIP: Mickey Hot Springs (12.6 miles; 1½ hours).
The road, which may be very dusty and bumpy, passes around Mickey Mountain. Watch for antelope ground squirrels and lizards. You pass areas of desert pavement and several playas. At Mickey Hot Springs (6.3) there are several beautiful glory pools, steam vents, and a boiling mud pot. Across the valley you can see the former shoreline of the lake that once occupied the Alvord Basin. The vicinity of the hot springs has rich populations of whiptails, leopard lizards, desert horned lizards, side-blotched lizards, and others. Rattlesnakes are also present. Watch for pronghorns and feral horses. Return to 8af.

8ag—Mann Lake Ranch (4.1). This large ranch dates back to 1871 and was formerly part of the Alvord Ranch. Note the "Western" mailbox.

8ah—Mann Lake (3.7). Provides excellent fishing for large rainbow and cutthroat trout and is a popular place for fishing through ice. Watch for pronghorns as you proceed.

8ai— Crested Wheatgrass Seeding (3.3). This area was burned by a range fire and seeded with crested wheatgrass to produce cattle forage.

8aj— Juniper Lake (7.7).

8ak—Juniper Lake Ranch (2.0). A large ranch that was established in 1874—once a part of John Devine's vast spread.

8al— Fifteen Cent Lake (3.8). Watch for shorebirds and water-fowl.

8am—Viewpoint (3.1). This prominence provides an excellent view of Steens Mountain and the Alvord Basin. Numerous small playas occur nearby.

8an— Follyfarm (1.0). A man named Neal attempted to farm here with irrigation, and the site was first called Neal's Folly, but later changed. A post office was established about 1909. Follyfarm is in Malheur County.

8ao— Highway 78 (3.3). Turn left to complete the tour; right to Winnemucca (157).

8ap—Viewpoint (7.0). From here one gets a good view of portions of the Harney Basin and of Virginia Valley.

8aq—Road to Malheur Cave (6.7). Turn right to take the side trip to Malheur Cave. Avoid this road after rains.

SIDE TRIP: Malheur Cave (6.0 miles; 2 hours).
The road has two forks—take the left road at each fork. If you explore the cave, take ample lights—preferably gas lanterns. See Chapter 10 for a detailed description. An old channel near the cave once drained the pluvial lake that filled the Harney Basin. A nearby reservoir is often visited by waterfowl, chukars, and quail; lizards are often seen in the area. Notice the abundance of obsidian flakes around the cave area. Return to 8aq.

8ar— Old Steam Channel (1.8). Here Highway 78 crosses the former channel that drained the great pluvial lake that filled the Harney Basin.

8as— Hat Butte (7.0). This interesting mesa (left) is surrounded by cliffs, consequently the top has not been grazed by cattle.

8at— Princeton (5.1). Turn left to return to Malheur Refuge or continue on Highway 78 to Burns (38).

8au— Diamond-Malheur Refuge Junction (3.2). Keep right, Continuing west, you will see irrigated land, crested wheatgrass seedings, desert shrubs, Malheur Lake marsh, and playas. Watch for pronghorns, coyotes, and other wildlife.

8av— Malheur Refuge (12). See 1g, Tour #1 and Chapter 10.

8aw—Malheur Field Station Road (3.0). Turn left to the Field Station (1.4) or continue straight to Highway 205 (3.2).

Tour #9

Tour: Northern Nevada
Route: Fields to Denio with options for through travel, side trips,

148

or returning to Fields.

Estimated Time: 2 hours

Distance: 39.2 miles (round trip to Denio Junction)

Hikes: Walk up Cottonwood Creek, climb the Pueblos, or select other hikes.

Starting Point: Fields, which can be reached by Tour #8 (see 8s) or by several other routes.

9a— From Fields the road follows the edge of the Alvord Basin and the foothills of the Pueblo Mountains. Desert shrubs and areas of bare desert pavement reflect the extreme aridity.

9b— Cottonwood Creek (8.1). This canyon is excellent birding (e.g., chukars, songbirds such as lazuli buntings, black-throated sparrows, etc.) and home for half a dozen species of lizards. Antelope ground squirrels and Mormon tea are also present. Don't try to drive more than a half mile—walk instead.

9c— Trout Creek Road (0.3). Turn left for a side trip up Trout Creek and to the Whitehorse Ranch.

SIDE TRIP: Trout Creek and the Whitehorse Ranch (52 miles; 4 hours).

After crossing the valley, the road follows Trout Creek, an excellent fishing stream (much of which is posted), and climbs up a narrow canyon with rugged rimrocks, talus slopes, and a rich growth of streamside vegetation. Chukars, quail, songbirds, and snakes may be seen. A few ranches, hay meadows, and abandoned buildings occur along the route. Eventually the road reaches a high desert valley, around the edges of which are white patches of diatomaceous earth. These yield large numbers of plant fossils (maples, oaks, etc.) and a few animal fossils as well. Obsidian is abundant along the road, and some large obsidian boulders can be found. Many feral horses live in this area. Watch for beaver sign where the road crosses Willow Creek. Not far beyond is the Whitehorse Ranch. Here on the abandoned site of Camp C.F. Smith, John Devine arrived in 1869 (see Chapter 3) to become the first permanent white settler in Harney County. Today the Whitehorse Ranch, larger than many small towns in the region, is arranged around Devine's famous barn. The white horse wind vane, high atop the magnificent old structure, is one of the best known historical landmarks in all of southeastern Oregon. From the ranch, one gets an interesting view of Steens Mountain and the vast empty space in between. One can continue to McDermitt or return to 9c and turn left.

9d— Tum Tum Lake (1.2). This lake, like many in the northern

Great Basin, is actually a dry playa most of the time. Interesting dust devils play over the playa when conditions are favorable. On the right, high upon the Pueblos are the roads and diggings of miners.

9e— Pueblo Mountains (2.9). Notice the various colors in the exposed rock. Bighorn sheep were released in the Pueblos in 1976. Ahead in the distance are the Pine Forest Mountains.

9f— Denio (Nevada Border) (9.3). Part of the town is in Oregon and part in Nevada.

9g— Diamond Bar (0.2). A famous refreshment spot, where you can meet local buckaroos in a Western atmosphere.

9h— Denio Junction (2.6). Through travelers can take Highway 140 south to Winnemucca (98) or west to Lakeview (127). If you are not interested in either of the side trips originating here, return to Fields (19.6) and resume Tour #8 at 8s.

SIDE TRIP: Bogue Hot (27.6 miles; 1 hour).
Turn right on Highway 140 and drive 9.3 miles to a junction. Along the way, observe the large playa and watch for antelope ground squirrels. Turn right at the junction and drive 3.7 miles to a pond on the left. Check the pond for waterfowl, wading birds, and shorebirds. Beyond the pond, take a left, which brings you to the Bogue Hot swimming hole. For most people, the water is too hot for daytime swimming. Walking upstream a short distance you will find a series of hot springs from which most of the hot water originates. Notice the colorful algae. Return to Highway 140 where you can take the side trip to Virgin Springs or return to Denio Junction.

SIDE TRIP: Virgin Springs (36.6 miles; 2 hours).
At Highway 140, turn right. Watch for pronghorns. Along the way notice the large flat-topped ridge on the right—an example of inverted topography (see the discussion of Wright's Point in Chapter 10). As you climb the grade, note the faults in the exposed sediments (13.0). Watch for burros in the valley below. Continue 3.3 miles, turn left and drive 2.5 miles to Virgin Springs Campground. Here there are several camp sites and public showers and swimming hole. Nearby ponds are well populated with a large number of species of birds, and bullfrogs may be heard calling at night. Colorful hills are found west of the campground, and a spectacular canyon is located a short distance northeast.

SIDE TRIP: Black Rock Desert
West of Denio on Highway 140, one can turn left and drive to

Summit Lake Indian Reservation, and continue east and south across the Black Rock Desert to Sulphur. Another road leads north to Quinn River Crossing on Highway 140. Other routes are available. Consult a good map and make inquiries locally about road conditions. This trip is recommended only for two or more well-equipped vehicles.

Tour #10

Tour: Strawberry Mountains
Route: Malheur Refuge north to Burns, Seneca, the Strawberry Wilderness Area, and back.
Estimated Time: A full day or two
Distance: 204.4 miles
Hikes: Many are available, e.g., climb Strawberry Peak, walk to High Lake, etc.
Starting Point: From Malheur Field Station or Malheur Refuge take Tour #5 to 5h and begin at that point.

10a— Junction of Highway 205 and the Double O Road. Drive toward Burns.

10b— Sunset Cemetery (6.2). On the right is a cemetery that grew during homesteading times when people lived nearby. The grave of Elkanah Peachwood, a child who died in 1845 on Meek's "lost wagon train" is said to have started the cemetery.

10c— Wright's Point (4.1). See Chapter 10 for an account of the geology.

10d— Viewpoint (0.7). Looking south one gets a good view of Steens Mountain, the Malheur Lake area, and other landscape. Descending the north side of Wright's Point, you see the Silvies floodplain and the Blue Mountains beyond. A large plume of smoke marks the site of the Edward Hines Lumber Mill.

10e— Silvies River (3.4). Here the highway crosses part of the Silvies River. Watch for birds as you proceed, especially at a large pond on the right.

10f— Squaw Butte Experiment Station (2.6). A facility devoted largely to cattle research, range management, and forage production.

10g— Highway 78 (4.8). At the junction, continue straight to reach Highway 20 or detour through Burns (where you may choose to visit the museum) and follow Highway 20 east to the point where Highway 395 begins (3.0).

10h— Highway 20 (2.0). Turn left and take Highway 395 (0.1).

10i— Juniper (3.8). Until now, the vegetation has consisted of desert shrubs, but here junipers begin to appear.

10j— Ponderosa Pine (4.7). A few scattered pines appear; farther on, pines become more dense and form a forest.

10k— Quaking Aspen (0.6). Aspen, willow, alder, and various species of riparian vegetation begin appearing in the canyon and along the stream. Notice the dogwood with bright red bark.

10l— Mountain Mahogany (0.6). This species appears on rocky, shallow soils.

10m—Idlewild Picnic Grounds (5.0). This pleasant roadside park is inhabited by an unusually large number of species of birds, including white-headed woodpeckers, crossbills, and many others. Several species of small mammals are also present.

10n—Bitterbrush (5.8). This important wildlife plant is abundant on the hill to the left. There is a nice stand of mountain mahogany across the road.

10o—Lone Pine (1.7). A stately large pine and its progeny make an unusual picture.

10p—Douglas Fir (0.9). Douglas fir begins to appear in protected ravines on the left.

10q—Silvies Valley (1.9). Here bison once roamed on lands belonging to the Ponderosa Wildlife Ranch, but the land is now used for cattle. Sandhill cranes, deer, and pronghorns may be seen as you proceed.

10r— Silvies (8.3). The original post office opened in 1892, but was later closed and reopened in the present location in 1915.

10s— Sagebrush (0.2). On the hills to the right, tall and short sagebrush grow together.

10t— Deer (1.1). Watch the willow thickets in the valley for deer.

10u— Willows on the Silvies River (5.8). The colorful bark of these willows and picturesque stream provide a beautiful view, especially during the winter.

10v— Seneca (3.1). Established in 1895, this logging town is best known for its cold winters and the Seneca Tavern, where the smell of sawdust on the floor add a genuine lumberjack atmosphere. From here, a side trip to Starr Campground begins. Turn right to Logan Valley for a continuation of the tour.

SIDE TRIP: Starr Campground (19.8 miles; 1½ hours).
Leaving Seneca, you get an excellent view of the Aldrich Mountains on the left and Strawberry Mountain on the right. Other picturesque scenery occurs along the way. At Starr Campground a diverse vegetation provides excellent habitat for

bird watching. If you drive beyond Starr Campground on Highway 395, you get a view of Canyon Creek Valley and the John Day country. Continue on to "Gold Country" or return to Seneca and turn left to continue the tour.

10w—Lodgepole pine (8.0). This species begins to appear here. Lodgepole pine has 2 needles per bundle.

10x—Larch (4.1). This conifer, sometimes called tamarack, has bundles of 14 to 30 needles borne on pegs on the branches. The clusters of needles, resembling old shaving brushes, are shed in the winter. The road bed near this location contains many large obsidian boulders.

10y—Junction (2.3). Turn left. Watch for game.

10z—Cattle Use (1.2). Note Bear Creek's width and depth, a result of cattle trampling the stream banks. Watch for ruffed grouse along the brushy edge of the stream.

10aa—Engelmann Spruce (1.5). Note the paper-like cones and prickly needles.

10ab—True Firs (1.8). White fir appears here. Watch for golden-mantled ground squirrels and red squirrels as you proceed.

10ac—Subalpine Firs (2.8). Observe the tall, spire shape, a useful growth form in areas of heavy snowfall. Watch for Columbian ground squirrels, elk, deer, bear, and other animals, including songbirds.

10ad—Junction (2.9). Stay left. Watch for Clark's nutcrackers.

10ae—White-barked Pine (0.3). Note the 5-needles per bundle, purple, pitch-covered cones, and characteristic bark color. Subalpine fir and lodgepole pine also occur here. Sagebrush continues to occur at this high elevation.

10af—Viewpoint (0.7). Climb to the top of the ridge on your right. Here you have a splendid view of a cirque valley, talus slopes, and the surrounding landscape. Clark's nutcrackers and golden-mantled ground squirrels are abundant. Please avoid disturbing the many wildflowers growing in the shallow soil.

10ag—Parking Place (0.3). From here you get a fantastic view of Strawberry Peak, other mountains, and the John Day Valley. The trail to Strawberry Peak begins at this point. Return to 10ad and turn left.

10ah—Parking Lot—High Lake (0.3). Examine the view of Bear Valley and Seneca. The trail to High Lake (1.0), which begins here, provides an unusual opportunity for one to view alpine plants, animals, and montane beauty. The cirque lake is stocked with Eastern brook trout and supports populations of spotted frogs and boreal toads. Return to 10y where you can turn left to Big Bend Campground, Prairie City, and on to "Gold Country", or turn right to return to Seneca, Burns, and Malheur Refuge.

Tour #11

Tour: Sage Grouse Lek (March 1 to May 10—or inquire).
Route: Malheur Field Station to the strutting ground and back.
Estimated Time: 2 to 3 hours. Be at the lek at sunrise, and **stay in your car!**
Distance: 47.4 miles
Starting Point: Malheur Field Station

11a—Drive north to the paved road that leads to Malheur Refuge Headquarters (1.4). Turn left.

11b—Highway 205 (3.2). Turn left.

11c—Foster Flat Road (10.8). Turn right. Stay on the main road, keeping right at all junctions. After 8 miles, begin watching for the grouse, especially on the left. The lek is at 8.3 miles from Highway 205. **Please stay in your car.** Watch for pronghorns, and feral horses. Take the same route back.

Appendix A

Directory

Highways

Several major highways converge upon Oregon's Great Basin country, giving through travelers a selection of routes. Most towns along highways are small, widely spaced, and often closed after dark. Check your road map for distances between services. Because of deer, horses, and cattle on roads, night driving can be hazardous.

U.S. Highway 20E—Bend to Burns (130 miles).

U.S. Highway 20W—Ontario to Burns (130 miles). This route crosses two mountain passes (4,200 and 4,800 feet elevation).

U.S. Highway 395S—Pendleton to John Day (120 miles); John Day to Burns (70 miles). This route crosses 5 mountain passes that range from 4,200 to 5,200 feet elevation.

U.S. 395N—Lakeview to Riley (113 miles); combined highways U.S. 20 and U.S. 395 to Burns (27 miles).

U.S. 95N—Winnemucca to Burns Junction (128 miles); Oregon Highway 78 from Burns Junction to Burns (92 miles). There are two passes higher than 5,000 feet.

U.S. Highway 95N— Winnemucca to the junction of Nevada Highway 140 (31 miles); Nevada Highway 140 to Denio Junction (66 miles); Nevada-Oregon Highway 205N to Frenchglen (78 miles). Highway 205 is an all-weather gravel road between Denio and the Roaring Springs Ranch in Catlow Valley, and crosses one pass (4,850 feet).

Roads

Most local roads are included in the recommended tours (Chapter 11).

Airports

Burns and Lakeview have municipal airports. Commercial flights (Air Oregon), charter service, and aviation fuel are available. Airstrips are located at Denio, Fields, Princeton, and at numerous other locations, but inquiries should be made before these strips are used.

Gas Stations

Complete automotive services are available in Burns, Hines, and Lakeview.

Gasoline is sold at the following locations: Adel, Brothers, Buchanan, Burns Junction, Crane, Denio, Denio Junction, Fields, Frenchglen, Hampton, Lawen, Millican, Plush, Princeton, Riley, Seneca, Silvies, and Wagontire. Other automotive services at these places range from fairly complete to none; many of the stations close at dark.

Information

Chamber of Commerce visitor centers are located in Burns and Lakeview. Other useful agencies include Hart Mountain National Antelope Refuge, the Malheur Field Station, Malheur National Wildlife Refuge, and offices of the Bureau of Land Management and U.S. Forest Service in Burns and Lakeview. Travel information is available at all small towns.

Lodging

Numerous motels are located in Burns, Hines, and Lakeview.

Denio, Denio Junction, and Fields have small motels, and there is a hotel in Frenchglen. The Malheur Field Station, with a capacity of 300, accepts large groups as well as small parties. Reservations should be made.

Trailer Courts

Hook-ups are available at Burns, Hines, Lakeview, Camper Corral (Frenchglen), and the Malheur Field Station. Trailers are permitted in several BLM and Forest Service campgrounds (e.g., Fish Lake, Page Springs, Starr, etc.), but there are no hook-ups.

Campgrounds

Big Bend (Logan Valley), Blitzen Crossing (Steens Mountain), Canyon Meadows (Canyon Creek), Delintment Lake (Ochoco National Forest), Fish Lake (Steens Mountain), Hot Spring (Hart Mountain National Antelope Refuge), Indian Springs (Strawberry Mountains), Jackman Park (Steens Mountain), Joaquin Miller (Malheur National Forest), Page Springs (Blitzen Valley), Parrish Cabin (Bear Valley), Starr (Malheur National Forest), Strawberry Lake (Strawberry Mountains), Virgin Springs (Sheldon National

Antelope Refuge), Wickiup (Canyon Creek), and Yellowjacket (Ochoco National Forest).

Idlewild (Malheur National Forest) can be used for picnicking only. Krumbo Reservoir (Malheur National Wildlife Refuge) accommodates self-contained campers and trailers.

Food Service

Various types of food services are available in Burns, Hines, and Lakeview. Restaurants are located at the Frenchglen Hotel (reservations required), Burns Junction, Denio Junction, Fields, and Wagontire.

Sandwiches are available in Denio (Diamond Bar), Princeton, and Seneca. Various types of snacks can be obtained in most small towns. Malheur Field Station serves meals to large groups (reservations required) and can often accept small groups on short notice—when the dining hall is in operation.

Groceries

Grocery stores vary from large, well-stocked shopping centers to tiny, one-room country stores. Stores are located in Adel, Buchanan, Burns, Crane, Denio Junction, Diamond, Fields, Frenchglen, Hines, Lakeview, Lawen, Plush, Princeton, Riley, Seneca, Silvies, and Wagontire.

Phone

Public phones are found in Buchanan, Burns, Denio, Frenchglen, Hines, Lakeview, Princeton, Riley, and Seneca. Usually local businesses, government agencies, and even private citizens will permit emergency use of telephones.

Auto Repair and Towing

These services are best obtained in larger centers such as Burns, Hines, and Lakeview. Flats and minor repairs are done at Buchanan, Denio, Denio Junction, Fields, Riley, and Seneca. Riley has towing service.

Hospital and Medical Services

Available only in Burns and Lakeview.

Post offices

Post offices are located in Adel, Burns, Crane, Diamond, Denio, Fields, Frenchglen, Hines, Lakeview, Plush, Princeton, Riley, Seneca, Silvies, and Wagontire.

Museums

Harney County Historical Museum (Burns), Malheur National Wildlife Refuge Museum—birds and mammals, Buchanan—a small display, primarily Indian artifacts.

Other

Newspapers, movies, libraries, state police, and other such services are found only in Burns and Lakeview.

Appendix B

The Origin of Selected Geographic Names

Adel. Formerly called Lonely (1891-1896). The name, possibly a woman's, is of uncertain origin.

Alberson. A post office (1907-1930) near Juniper Lake; named for a local settler.

Alvord. A name applied to numerous geographical features in southern Harney County; honors Brigadier-General Benjamin Alvord, a prominent military figure in early Oregon.

Andrews. An abandoned post office, named for a local resident.

Baca Lake. From Vaca, Spanish for cow; currently spelled Boca Lake.

Barton Lake. Named for a local settler.

Beaty Butte. Honors Sergeant A.M. Beaty, member of a calvary troop that came through in 1864.

Beckley. A former post office in the Catlow Valley; named for a local resident.

Berdugo. A former post office near Roaring Springs, in the Catlow Valley; named for one of Peter French's vaqueros.

Blitzen. German for lightning.

Bluejoint Lake. One of the many lakes in Warner Valley; refers to a type of local grass.

Buchanan. A local family name.

Buena Vista. Spanish for beautiful view.

Burns. Called Axe Handle until 1884; the current name honors Robert Burns, the Scottish poet.

Camp C.F. Smith. Established in 1866 at the present site of the Whitehorse Ranch; the name honors a prominent military officer.

Camp Currey. Established in 1865 on Silver Creek; named for Colonel George B. Currey.

Camp Warner. Established in 1866, but actually occupied two locations; named for Captain W.H. Warner who was killed by Indians in 1849.

Camp Wright. Established near the present location of the Island Ranch in 1865; named for Brigadier-General George Wright.

Canyon City. Originally called Whiskey Gulch; located in a narrow canyon.

Catlow Valley. Named for an early stockman and businessman.

Chewaucan Marsh. From the Indian word for wild potato, i.e., wapato or *Sagittaria*.

Crane. Refers to the presence of sandhill cranes or other large birds in the area.

Cucamonga Creek. A name borrowed from southern California by Dolly Kiger.

Del Norte. A former post office near Saddle Butte on the north side of Malheur Lake; Spanish for "from the north".

Denio. For Aaron Denio, who settled nearby in 1885.

Diamond. A name applied to several geographical features including the community, which was named in 1874; refers to the brand used by Mace McCoy.

Donner und Blitzen River. German for thunder and lightning; named in 1864 by Colonel G.B. Currey; formerly called the New River.

Double O Ranch. Refers to the OO brand.

Drewsey. Originally Gouge Eye, then Drusy, and later Drewsey— a woman's name.

Fields. Fomerly Field's Station; named for a local homesteader.

Fort Harney. Established in 1867 as Camp Steele, later called Camp Harney, then Harney. Named for Major-General W.S. Harney.

Fort Rock. A prominent rocky landmark and a famous archeological site.

Frenchglen. Called Somerange until 1930; honors Peter French and Dr. Hugh Glenn.

Glass Butte. Abundant obsidian or volcanic glass.

Goose Lake. Formerly Pit Lake; refers to waterfowl use.

Grant County. Established in 1864; named for General U.S. Grant.

Guano Lake and Creek. Named in 1864; refers to guano deposits.

Happy Valley. A tribute to the disposition of the local residents.

Harney. Many geographic features bear names honoring Brigadier-General William S. Harney. Harney County was established in 1889. Harney Lake had former names such as Salt Lake, Bitter Lake, etc., before Captain Wallace named it for Harney in 1859.

Hart Mountain, etc. Named for the heart brand used on a nearby ranch; the misspelling is now accepted.

Hines. Originally called Egan for the Paiute chief, later changed to Herrick, and then Hines when the mill was bought by the Edward Hines Lumber Company.

Howluk Butte. Named for a Paiute chief by Major Enoch Steen; located 2 miles east of Alvord Lake.

Iron Mountain. First called Pleasanton Butte, renamed for the appearance of the rocks.

Island Ranch. Surrounded by tributaries of the Silvies River.

Izee. Refers to the IZ brand.

John Day. A member of the Astor-Hunt party (1810-1812).

Jackman Park. E.R. Jackman was an author and well-known agricultural extension agent.

Kiger Gorge and Creek. Named for a local pioneer family.

Krumbo Creek and Reservoir. Named for an early resident in the area.

Lake Abert. First called Salt Lake; renamed for Colonel J.J. Abert by John Fremont.

Lake County. Established in 1874; named for its many lakes.

La Mu. A former post office near the present location of Crane; the name's origin is a mystery.

Lawen. Probably a misspelled honor for Henry Lauen, a local settler.

Loma. A former post office about 8 miles north of Narrows; Spanish for rising ground.

Lonely. See Adel.

Malheur. A commonly used name in the region; derived from the French word for "unfortunate", in reference to lost goods stolen by Indians. Malheur Lake had several previous names.

Mann Lake. Named for a local rancher.

McCoy Creek. Named for Mace McCoy, a rancher in the area.

Mugwump Lake. A lake in the Warner Valley; name describes its unpredictable changes from wet to dry.

Narrows. First called Springer for a local resident; describes the narrow connecting waterway between Malheur and Mud lakes.

Oroville. Site of a former post office 5 miles south of Fields; Oro means gold in Spanish, a reference to nearby mining activity.

P Ranch. Peter French's headquarters; named for the P brand that French bought from Porter.

Plush. The name is said to commemorate an Indian poker player's pronunciation of "flush".

Poison Creek. A name given when cattle died; probably not from the water, but from eating poison hemlock.

Princeton. Named for Princeton, Mass. by an early settler in the area.

Pueblo Mountain. Spanish for town; apparently refers to the mining community established there about 1863. A Paiute name for the mountain means "sitting solid".

Riddle Mountain and Creek. Named for a local settler.

Riley. Named for an early rancher.

Roaring Springs. Probably refers to the sound of water cascading down the slope.

Saddlebutte. A former post office near Saddle Butte, on the northeast shore of Malheur Lake.

Sage Hen Creek. A reference to sage grouse.

Sageview. A post office in Catlow Valley from 1916-1918.

Seneca. Named in 1895 for a Portland judge, Seneca Smith.

Serrano Point. Spanish for mountaineer.

Shirk. A former post office near Home Creek; named for a pioneer family in the area.

Silver Creek. May have come from mistaking the creek for the Silvies River.

Silvies River. Antoine Sylvaille was sent to the area by Peter Skeene Ogden and discovered the river in 1826. In 1860, Enoch Steen renamed it the Cricket River, but Sylvaille prevailed and was eventually shortened to Silvies.

Smyth Creek. Named for D.H. Smyth, a pioneer whose father and brother were killed in Happy Valley in 1878 by Indians.

Sod House. Refers to the structure built in 1862 near the site of Malheur Refuge Headquarters; two sets of brothers spent the winter there.

Somerange. Means summer range; see Frenchglen.

Steens Mountain. Originally named Snow Mountain by John Work in 1831; renamed for Major Enoch Steen who pursued Indians there in 1860.

Strawberry Mountain. Called Logan Butte, Strawberry Butte, and finally Strawberry Mountain, a name relating to the presence of wild strawberries.

Summer Lake. When John Fremont stood on Winter Ridge on a cold, stormy day the greenery of the valley below reminded him of summer.

Thelake. A post office from 1914 to 1918 near Mann Lake.

Three Mile Creek. Three miles south of Home Creek.

Tiara. Means head ornament; a post office located at the head (north end) of Catlow Valley from 1916 to 1917.

Venator. Named for a prominent early settler.

Voltage. A former post office near headquarters of Malheur Wildlife Refuge; the first postmaster was fascinated by electricity.

Wagontire. Formerly called Egli for a local rancher; Indians burned a wagon and a metal tire lay near the road.

Warner Valley. Named for Captain W.H. Warner, who was killed by Indians in 1849. Warner Mountain is now called Hart Mountain. There are 11 lakes in Warner Valley, but none is called Warner Lake.

Whitehorse Ranch. In 1868 when John Devine established his ranch on the former site of Camp C.F. Smith, he named it Whitehorse after a nearby creek that was named in 1866 or before. The name may have referred to a magnificent white horse ridden by an Indian chief in the area.

Whorehouse Meadows. Women from Vale set up shop in tents and ministered to the desires of Steens Mountain cattlemen and sheepmen. Attempts of moralists to change the name to Naughty Girl Meadows have fortunately failed.

Windy. A designated post office, near Windy Point east of Malheur Lake, which failed to open because of competition from the nearby Waverly post office (also defunct).

Winter Ridge. The weather was winter-like as John Fremont stood here and looked down upon Summer Lake.

Wright's Point. Named for Brigadier-General George Wright.

Selected Readings and References

Advisory Committee on Predator Control. 1972. *Predator Control—1971.* Institute for Environmental Quality, University of Michigan, Ann Arbor, Michigan. 207 p.

Bailey, Vernon. 1936. *The Mammals and Life Zones of Oregon.* United States Department of Agriculture, Washington, D.C. 416 p.

Baldwin, Ewart M. 1964. *Geology of Oregon.* Edwards Brothers, Ann Arbor, Michigan. 165 p.

Bond, Carl, E. 1973. *Keys to Oregon Freshwater Fishes.* Oregon State University, Corvallis, Oregon. 42 p.

Brimlow, George F. 1951. *Harney County, Oregon and Its Range Land.* Binfords and Mort, Portland, Oregon. 316 p.

Brogan, Phil F. 1964. *East of the Cascades.* Binfords and Mort, Portland, Oregon. 304 p.

Brown, G.W. (Ed.). 1968. *Desert Biology.* Acadamic Press, New York, New York. 635 p.

Burt, William H., and Richard P. Grossenheider. 1964. A Field *Guide to the Mammals.* Houghton Mifflin, Boston, Massachusetts. 284 p.

Cahalane, Victor H. 1947. *Mammals of North America.* Macmillan, New York, New York, 682 p.

Conkling, Charles, E.R. Jackman, and John Scharff. 1967. *Steens Mountain.* Caxton Printers, Caldwell, Idaho. 203 p.

Craighead, John J., Frank C. Craighead, and Roy J. Davis. 1963. *A Field Guide to Rocky Mountain Wildflowers.* Houghton Mifflin, Boston, Massachusetts. 277 p.

Cronquist, Arthur, Arthur H. Holmgren, Noel H. Holmgren, and James L. Reveal. 1972. *Intermountain Flora [Vol. 1].* Hafner Publishing Company, New York, New York. 270 p.

Dicken, Samuel N. 1973. *Oregon Geography.* Edwards Brothers, Ann Arbor, Michigan. 147 p.

Ekman, Leonard C. 1962. *Scenic Geology of the Pacific Northwest.* Binfords and Mort, Portland, Oregon. 310 p.

French, Giles, 1964. *The Cattle Country of Peter French.* Binfords and Mort, Portland, Oregon. 167 p.

Gabrielson, Ira N., and Stanley G. Jewett. 1940. *Birds of Oregon.* Oregon State University, Corvallis, Oregon. 650 p.

Hadley, Neil F. (Ed.). 1975. *Environmental Physiology of Desert Organisms*. Dowden, Hutchinson, and Ross, Stroudsbury, Pennsylvania. 283 p.

Hanley, Mike. 1973. *Owyhee Trails*. Caxton Printers, Caldwell, Idaho. 314 p.

Highsmith, Richard M., and Robert Bard. 1973. *Atlas of the Pacific Northwest*. Oregon State University, Corvallis, Oregon. 128 p.

Hitchcock, C. Leo, and Arthur Cronquist. 1973. *Flora of the Pacific Northwest*. University of Washington Press, Seattle, Washington. 730 p.

Hubbard, Larry L. 1975. *Hydrology of Malheur Lake, Harney County, Southeastern Oregon*. U.S. Geological Survey, Portland, Oregon. 40 p.

Ingram, D.L., and L.E. Mount. 1975. *Man and Animals In Hot Environments*. Springer-Verlag, New York, New York. 185 p.

Jackman, E.R., and R.A. Long. 1971. *The Oregon Desert*. Caxton Printers, Caldwell, Idaho. 407 p.

Jackson, Donald D. 1975. *Sagebrush Country*. Time-Life Books. New York, New York. 184 p.

Kirk, Ruth, 1965. *Exploring Death Valley*. Stanford University Press, Stanford, California. 88 p.

Kirk, Ruth. 1973. *Desert*. Houghton Mifflin, Boston, Massachusetts. 361 p.

Klingeman, P.C., et. al. 1971. *Environmental Considerations and the Water Resources of the Silvies Basin*. Water Resources Research Institute, Oregon State University, Corvallis, Oregon. 49 p. + Appendices A-G.

Larrison, Earl J., 1976. *Mammals of the Northwest*. Seattle Audubon Society, Seattle, Washington. 256 p.

Loy, William G., 1976. *Atlas of Oregon*. University of Oregon Books, Eugene, Oregon. 215 p.

McArthur, Lewis A. 1974. *Oregon Geographic Names*. Oregon Historical Society, Portland, Oregon. 835 p.

McKee, Bates. 1972. *Cascadia*. McGraw-Hill, New York, New York. 394 p.

Neihaus, Theodore F., and Charles L. Ripper. 1976. *A Field Guide to Pacific States Wildflowers*. Houghton Mifflin, Boston, Massachusetts. 432 p.

Oliver, Herman. 1961. *Gold and Cattle Country*. Binfords and Mort, Portland, Oregon. 312 p.

Patton, Clyde P., Charles S. Alexander, and Fritz L. Kramer. 1970. *Physical Geography*. Wadsworth, Belmont, California. 408 p.

Peterson, Roger T. 1969. *A Field Guide to Western Birds.* Houghton Mifflin, Boston, Massachusetts. 366 p.

Peck, Morton E. 1941. *A Manual of the Higher Plants of Oregon.* Binfords and Mort, Portland, Oregon. 866 p.

Pimentel, Richard A. 1967. *Natural History.* Reinhold Publishing Corporation, New York, New York. 436 p.

Schmidt-Nielsen, Knut. 1965. *Desert Animals.* Oxford University Press, London. 277 p.

State Water Resources Board. 1967. *Malheur Lake Basin.* State Water Resources Board, Salem, Oregon. 110 p.

Stebbins, Robert C. 1966. *A Field Guide to Western Reptiles and Amphibians.* Houghton Mifflin, Boston, Massachusetts. 279 p.

Taylor, Ronald J., and Rolf W. Valum. 1974. *Wildflowers 2: Sagebrush Country.* Touchstone Press, Beaverton, Oregon. 143 p.

U.S. Department of Agriculture. 1941. *Climate and Man.* United States Government Printing Office, Washington, D.C. 1248 p.

Voigt, William. 1976. *Public Grazing Lands.* Rutgers University Press, New Brunswick, New Jersey. 359 p.

Wheat, Margaret M. 1967. *Survival Arts of the Primitive Paiutes.* University of Nevada Press, Reno, Nevada. 117 p.

Index

171

Notes